PSYCHOLOGY PRACTITIONER GUIDEBOOKS

EDITORS

Arnold P. Goldstein, Syracuse University
Leonard Krasner, Stanford University & SUNY at Stony Brook
Sol L. Garfield, Washington University in St. Louis

SCHOOL CONSULTATION

Titles of Related Interest

SCHOOL CONSULTATION
Practice and Training,
Second Edition

JANE CLOSE CONOLEY
COLLIE W. CONOLEY
University of Nebraska-Lincoln

Allyn and Bacon
Boston • London • Toronto • Sydney • Tokyo • Singapore

ISBN 0-205-14561-2

Printed in the United States of America

98 97   10 9 8 7 6

Library of Congress Cataloging in Publication Data

Conoley, Jane Close.
    School consultation : practice and training / Jane Close Conoley,
Collie W. Conoley. -- 2nd ed.
    . p.   cm. -- (Psychology practitioner guidebooks)
    Includes index.
    1. School psychology--United States. 2. Psychological
consultation. I. Conoley, Collie W. (Collie Wyatt), 1949–
II. Title. III. Series.
LB1027.55.C66   1991
370.15--dc20   90-27472
                                            CIP

The paper used in this publication meets the minimum requirements of American
National Standard for Information Sciences—Permanence of Paper for Printed
Library Materials, ANSI Z39.48-1984

To our friends,
all people with special understanding.

Contents

Preface

In 1982 we described the first edition of this volume as merely a beginning. Writing the second edition has not changed this perception. Despite 8 years of additional study and practice, we are still amazed that there is so much to learn about the process of helping others do their work in more satisfying ways.

We know that doing consultation with the excitement of a believer and the caution and skepticism of a behavioral scientist is the best teacher. Individuals must be experts in something before they begin their consultation careers. In addition, they must care deeply about using their knowledge to help others. Risk taking, common sense, knowledge, and compassion are necessary for effective consultation. Once these skills are in place, the consultant is ready for action.

The school is the primary avenue to all children and most families. Consultants serious about the delivery of psychological services must see the school, fraught as it is with conflicting missions, as the most desirable work site for people committed to child welfare. Only the most effective people can make meaningful contributions while simultaneously dealing with difficult organizational issues.

For these reasons, we decided to write a second edition. This new volume is changed in some superficial and some substantive ways from the first edition. We have minimized theoretical models as organizing devices because we find that a more ecological model now guides our work and research. We have given greater emphasis to increasing the acceptability of interventions, intervention assistance teams, and ethics. Advocacy consultation is included as an element of ecological work, not as a separate model. This will delight some readers and dismay others but does not indicate less devotion to the ideals of advocacy, just a more pragmatic organizational scheme.

This edition is written with practitioner needs at the forefront. Since the publication of the first edition in 1982, both of us have been involved heavily in practice. We have tried to incorporate lessons from this experience in this edition. We have written this book for psychologists, special educators, school social workers, counselors, and administrators. All of our examples involve schools. Those who work in other settings will find the general principles applicable to consultation practice in any setting. We decided, however, to focus on the school setting because children are there for thousands of hours during their formative years.

To address the needs of practitioners, the information is focused on necessary skills, pragmatic ways of evaluating effectiveness, typical obstacles or roadblocks to success, special considerations associated with entry into organizations, and the pervasive role that ethics plays in consultation practice. Although we incorporate the latest research in our presentations, we do not provide an exhaustive review of research. The suggested readings and reference sections will be a useful guide to those interested in more in-depth research investigation.

Jane Close Conoley and Collie W. Conoley
1990

Acknowledgments

Our colleagues at the University of Nebraska at Lincoln deserve special notice for providing an environment that supports scholarly endeavor and is characterized by close collegial relationships. We thank our colleagues in the departments of Educational Psychology, Psychology, and Communication Disorders and Special Education, as well as our Dean, for their unfailing good humor and encouragement. The people in Nebraska and nationwide who have invited us to be involved with them professionally in difficult organizational and child welfare issues have made indelible impressions on our work. Each individual consultee and host agency has been important to us. This is equally true of our students. We learn as much as we teach from them. Jerry Frank of Pergamon Press was patient beyond the bounds of human expectations, and we are forever grateful to him. Finally, although our family has changed in the last 8 years, the special place occupied by our children, Brian, Colleen, and Collin, has remained constant. They are the source of our will to improve situations that children and their caregivers face. We marvel at our children's uniqueness and are thankful that we are a family.

Chapter 1

Definition and Purpose of Consultation

WHAT IS CONSULTATION?

Consultation is a voluntary, nonsupervisory relationship between professionals from differing fields designed to aid professional functioning. The rationale for a mental health professional (consultant) spending time with a teacher, minister, or probation officer (consultee), instead of with the child, parishioner, or prisoner (client), is based on efficiency, impact, and prevention considerations.

The consultant hopes that the consultee will generalize the insights and skills learned in the discussion of a single client case to other clients under the care of the consultee. Such generalization suggests the efficiency of consultation.

The rationale regarding impact is that clients are best treated by those who have long-duration or high-intensity contact with them. Because most specialists have adopted some organizational variation of the 50-minute-hour weekly treatment modality, the most highly trained specialists may spend limited time with those they were trained to serve. The regular caregivers (e.g., parents, teachers, day-care workers, principals) in a client's life should be shown how to facilitate problem solving with clients because they spend the most time with the clients.

In addition, if generalization and transfer of skills occur because of consultation, there is potential for the primary prevention of adjustment problems (e.g., learning, behavior, personal interactions, attitudes). The possibility of using consultation as a preventive intervention is encouraging. Rudimentary reports that appear in the literature lend some credence to consultation's prevention potential (e.g., Conoley & Conoley, 1982; Meyers, 1975; Ritter, 1978).

1

A summary of the important parameters of consultation services is as follows:

1. The consultee initiates the service.
2. The consultee has complete freedom to accept or reject consultation services.
3. The relationship is confidential.
4. The relationship is characterized as among peer professionals and is collaborative and coordinate.
5. The relationship provides resources to children's caregivers in a cost-effective way.
6. The relationship deals only with professional problems.
7. The focus is on prevention.
8. The consultant's goals are as follows:
    a. Provide an objective point of view.
    b. Increase problem-solving skills.
    c. Facilitate coping skills.
    d. Expand freedom of choice.
    e. Enhance commitment to choices made.
    f. Increase resources available for handling persistent problems.

WHAT CONSULTATION IS NOT

The term *consultation* has been applied to so many professional functions that it may be useful to define consultation further by mentioning what it is not. For example, consultants differ from supervisors, program developers, collaborators, teachers, and psychotherapists, but they do some of the tasks of each. Some of these similarities and differences are discussed next.

Supervision

Supervisors give advice and are interested in supporting the work of their supervisees. In this way they are similar to consultants. In addition, supervisors are usually the primary source of evaluative data about supervisees.

Supervision requirements usually include mandatory meetings and acceptance of supervisors' suggestions. Supervisors make decisions about the careers of their subordinates: hiring, firing, raises, promotions, and so on. Inherent in the supervisory role, therefore, are certain facets that may make honest self-disclosure about work performance difficult for the supervisee. The supervisory role also contains elements that make it difficult for the supervisor to adopt an accepting, developmental stance toward supervisee difficulties. The supervisor if often ultimately responsible for the supervisee's work. This responsibility can make supervisors directive.

The wise consultant, therefore, avoids some supervisory functions to facilitate a mutually beneficial relationship with the consultee. Such functions include evaluative comments, reporting career-relevant data to consultees' supervisors, insisting that recommendations be followed (even if only indirectly), and overly structuring the amount of meeting time or content of meetings (see Fuchs & Fuchs, 1989, for another viewpoint). In subsequent discussions of ethics, however, the lines between supervision and consultation may be diffuse in certain situations.

Program Development

When new programs (e.g., computer-assisted instruction, values clarification, behavior modification, or student assistance teams) are introduced into an organization, consultants are often hired to enhance the implementation. If people are selling a particular technology, they are not consultants. If they are helping an organization decide what fits its needs and use whatever new technologies have been jointly chosen, they are consulting.

Consultants sell their problem-solving services. Program developers sell their problem-solving services and a particular product. Along with offering a service, the initial concern of the program developer is to convince the potential customer or consultee that the product being sold is right for whatever client or organizational problem has been identified. For the program developer, the problem must lead to the product being sold.

Every consultant has a limited repertoire of responses for a particular consultee concern. The best consultants do not know everything but also do not close their minds to any potential solutions. Program developers may not attend to certain alternatives while promoting the options that sell their product.

Collaboration

Professional collaboration involves sharing the work and responsibility for some activity. Consultation theorists differ on the limits of collaboration in a consulting relationship. Caplan (1970) described mental health consultation as a situation in which the consultant provides no direct service to clients; that is, it is a coordinate but not collaborative relationship. Others conceptualize consultation applications in which the consultant implements part of the remedial plan or views himself or herself as partially accountable for the results of the consultation (Bergan, 1977; Bergan & Kratochwill, 1990; Idol, Paolucci-Whitcomb, & Nevin, 1986; Meyers, 1973).

An important element that differentiates the two perspectives is the goals of consultation. If active participation in an intervention results in consultee dependency and no new skills, collaboration would be a mistake. If, however, working side by side is seen as a way to model skills, increase behavioral repertoires, ensure first-attempt successes, or show concern and investment, then collaboration is consistent with consultation goals. Practically speaking, however, to increase efficiency, only so much collaboration can be done. The skills of knowing how much involvement to offer and how to fade out of implementation plans are important.

Teaching

Teaching is a process of imparting a specified body of information in a planned, systematic way. Consultants impart information, but do so in response to consultee need. Consultants engage in problem-solving steps but rarely in organized curricula.

Although they must be mindful always of ethical considerations (i.e., consultants must be competent in the areas in which they work), consultants will not be helpful if they are experts in only a narrow range of techniques (e.g., behavior modification or psychoanalysis) or if they are willing to address only a child's academic difficulties while screening out emotional or social concerns. Depending on the setting and content areas in which consultants specialize, a broad and general understanding of organizational members' issues is helpful.

Consultants, like teachers, must be aware of the many ways in which teaching is accomplished. Modeling, relationship building, nonverbal reactions, specific problem formulations, and presentation of alternative worldviews may be helpful. All of these are discussed later in this book.

Psychotherapy

Psychotherapy, with its emphasis on helping people adjust, opening up new cognitive and behavioral alternatives, and developing beneficial relationships, is similar to consultation. Therapy, however, also involves probing for personal emotional information over a broad spectrum of the patient's life situation, past and present.

Therapist and patient must at some point agree that the patient has a problem that requires some personality or behavior change. Most therapies (but not behavior therapy) seek to weaken a patient's defensive structures (e.g., denial, rationalization, projection) so more valid information is available for conscious interpretation. Consultation, on the other hand, limits the focus to problems experienced by consultees in their work settings, does not involve much emotional probing (certainly none about a consultee's past emotional history), and generally works to keep the consultee from experiencing a loss of typical coping patterns.

Psychotherapy patients often report a crisis phase in which they are unable to integrate new insights with old behaviors and attitudes. They have a tendency to experience intense dependency on the therapist. Consultants, while working to add to a consultee's behavioral repertoire and provide new ways of seeing old problems, do not wish to throw a consultee into a crisis that demands continuous consultant support. Consultants must remain alert to the possibility that consultees will be vulnerable and in need of psychotherapy. Appropriate referral skills and sources are necessary.

USEFUL THEORIES

Whenever consultants choose how to approach an angry parent, underachieving child, or disgruntled organizational member, they are making use of a theory of human behavior. Theories people use may differ from theories they espouse intellectually. The familiar expression "do what I say, not what I do" reflects the distance between what people say they believe and how they actually behave. This distance may account for the fairly widespread disdain for theory that is evident among practitioners of many professions. "Don't talk theory," students often implore. "Tell us how to do consultation, not what people think about it."

Recent evidence from cognitive psychology lends support to students' pleas. People seem to learn by doing, not by learning general principles about something (Tharp & Gallimore, 1985) That is, they often *know how* without *knowing what.*

The prominent theories in consultation literature can be analyzed using action criteria. In this way, the how and the what may be combined. For example, how does believing in the unconscious change the way a consultant approaches a consultee? How does conceptualizing mainly external motivators limit or enhance the selection of consultation targets? If process events in the environment are seen to be of prime importance, in what initial activities should a consultant engage?

Three theoretical perspectives are preeminent in consultation. These are mental health consultation (Caplan, 1970; Meyers, Parsons, & Martin, 1979), behavioral consultation (Bergan, 1977; Bergan & Kratochwill, 1990; Bergan & Neumann, 1980; Bergan & Tombari, 1976), and process consultation (Schein, 1969; Schmuck & Runkel, 1985). These differ from each other in many ways but especially in terms of how environmental influence is conceptualized. (See Table 1.1.)

Collaborative consultation, instructional consultation, and problem-solving approaches have received significant attention (Fuchs & Fuchs, 1989; Gutkin & Curtis, 1990; Idol, Nevin, & Paolucci-Whitcomb, 1986; Idol, Paolucci-Whitcomb, & Nevin, 1986; Pryzwansky, 1974, 1977; Rosenfield, 1987). These do not represent additional theories of consultation,

Table 1.1. Internal and External Focus of Major Perspectives in Consultation.

Mental Health Consultation	Process Consultation	Behavioral Consultation
Internal forces (e.g., attitudes, motivation, irrational thoughts)	Interactive forces (e.g., communication, leadership, interpersonal relations)	External forces (e.g., environment, punishments, rewards)

however, but refinements concerning the consultation relationship and an application of consultation in a particular content area. West and Idol (1987) provided an exhaustive review of consultation theory and should be studied by those interested in a sophisticated analysis of theory building.

In the following sections, each of the major consultation approaches is analyzed according to the following action criteria: (a) How is consultation best introduced? (b) Who is the target of service? (c) What strategies flow from particular perspectives? and (d) How is work evaluated for effectiveness?

Mental Health Consultation

This is the prototypic consultation approach. It has the longest history and is based on the most traditional psychological understandings of human behavior. Developed in the 1960s by psychiatrist Gerald Caplan (1970), mental health consultation was a revolutionary step away from classical Freudian or psychodynamic psychology. Caplan proposed that caregiver consultees' (e.g., teachers, nurses, probation officers, ministers) job effectiveness could be enhanced through a coordinate process of case discussion and problem solving with a consultant. He also suggested that consultants pay close attention to the organizational realities of their consultation settings and concentrate on the relationships among people rather than on the intrapsychic difficulties that might be uncovered.

Caplan conceptualized caregivers' difficulties as stemming from lack of skills, knowledge, self-esteem, or professional objectivity. Although Caplan was a revolutionary, he was still dynamically oriented. He hypothesized and presented supportive evaluative evidence that most consultees have work difficulties due to problems in professional objectivity. He asserted that such difficulties must be handled through delicate and covert verbal strategies.

Subsequent research has cast doubt on Caplan's predictions of the source of consultee difficulties (Gutkin, 1981). In consultation, as in any other endeavor, people tend to find what they are looking for (Kelly, 1963;

Salmon & Lehrer, 1989). Gutkin's experimenter-consultants, trained in behavioral consultation, were likely to see consultees' lack of overt skills and behaviors, while Caplan's (1970) psychiatrists were likely to emphasize unconscious dynamics in their case reports. Because Caplan considered losses in professional objectivity to be the most common causes of consultee difficulty, his most important mental health consultation intervention was aimed at reducing just that problem. Theme interference was the term he used to describe consultees' unconscious link with a particular case causing unusual ineffectiveness. Theme interference reduction is the strategy to help consultees break loose of constricting thoughts or feelings about a particular client or issue.

Entry Issues. A major contribution of this perspective is the recognition that not all consultee behavior is rationally or consciously motivated. Consultees do become overly identified with their clients (e.g., children, work problems, customers), they do become angry while denying anger as a possibility, and, at times, consultees need emotional support as much or more than they need answers.

Introducing mental health consultation to an organization may be difficult. The techniques used by the consultant may seem rather vague to an administrator (indirect confrontation, support, theme interference), the time frames associated with noticeable improvement in consultee or client performance are impossible to specify, and explaining mental health consultation to consultees is problematic. Seymour Sarason's entry speech in a school setting is still applicable to these concerns (Sarason, Levine, Goldenberg, Cherlin, & Bennett, 1960).

> When we say we want to be helpful in . . . the school, we mean that in addition to talking with the teacher about a child, *we have to be able to observe that child in the context of the classroom in which the problem manifests itself.* For help to be meaningful and practical it must be based on what actually goes on in the classroom setting. . . . We do not view ourselves in the schools as people to whom questions are directed and from whom answers will be forthcoming. . . . We have no easy answers, but we have a way of functioning that involves us in a relationship with the teacher and the classroom and that together we can come up with concrete ideas and plans that we feel will be helpful to a particular child. . . . I hope I have made clear that when we say we want to help it means that we want to talk to the teacher, observe in the classroom, talk again to the teacher, and together come up with a plan of action that with persistence, patience, and consistency gives promise of bringing about change. It is not a quick process and it is certainly not an easy one. (pp. 58–62)

Agency administrators often understand that some of their staff's problems with clients are due to staff difficulties; for example, that teachers lack knowledge of particular teaching strategies. Administrators may be befud-

dled, however, by the suggestion that a relationship process like consultation is necessary to improve teacher skills. They are more likely to believe
that in-service training, supervision, and more effort on the part of the
teacher are the predictors of improvement.

Most consultees accept that they make some contribution to the failures
they experience in their professional functioning, but admitting such contributions is threatening. Consultation must be explained to them in such
a way that the threat of having another adult involved with them in their
difficulties is reduced (Friend, 1984, 1985). According to Sarason,

> I cannot state too strongly that we are not coming into the schools with the
> intent of criticizing or passing judgement on anyone. *We are nobody's private FBI
> or counterintelligence service. We are not the agent of the principal or some other administrative
> office.* (Sarason et al., 1960, p.61)

Targets. Although mental health consultants have diverse goals, they work
primarily to improve client gains. To accomplish such an improvement,
however, mental health consultants most often work with the consultees
(teachers, therapists, ministers). Given the assumption that at least some
of clients' difficulties are exacerbated by caregiver characteristics (or characteristics of other significant relationships), consultants target working
with caregivers. Their direct work with clients is done only to model more
appropriate styles or strategies, or to accomplish some diagnostic procedures. This caregiver-focused service is clearly the most reasonable approach (see Conoley & Gutkin, 1986a; Gutkin & Conoley, 1990) but creates difficulties with consultees who would like the consultants to take
clients away, fix them, and then (and *only* then) send them back.

Consultants can choose among four variants of mental health consultation: client centered, consultee centered, program, and administrative consultation. Further, consultants must decide if the program or administrative work will be mainly client or consultee centered. These distinctions
refer to goals and major targets for change. Client-centered approaches are
used when a consultee lacks information. The focus is on the case as
defined by the consultee and consultant. In the consultee-centered approaches, however, the consultant determines that consultee skills, objectivity, or self-esteem are interfering with work performance and so emphasizes working with the consultee. The case, administrative issue, or
program is used merely as a vehicle to assist the consultee.

The consultant must retain the flexibility of moving among the mental
health models as the situation demands. This presupposes, however, that
the consultant is constantly conceptualizing and testing hypotheses about
the sources of the problem between the consultee and the client.

Strategies. The key strategies used by mental health consultants include
sophisticated diagnostic formulations, theme interference reduction, rela-

tionship building, and onedownsmanship. Because mental health consultants view their consultees' emotional lives as crucial in explaining the consultees' work effectiveness, consultants must be talented in discerning what is blocking the consultees' problem-solving skills. Is it simply lack of knowledge or skills? If this is the case, the consultant can supply information or model skills. Is the problem due to poor confidence or self-esteem? If so, the accepting, egalitarian relationship offered to the consultee will improve the situation.

Are the problems due to theme interference? A theme is an unconscious formulation by the consultee that inhibits problem solving. For example, a teacher who is having serious trouble disciplining his adolescent daughter may experience difficulty in managing a student who resembles the daughter. He may be unaware of the connection, or aware but unable to change the situation. The consultant can show respect for the consultee's ideas and opinions, thus increasing the consultee's self-confidence. In addition, the consultant can point out all the other young female students being taught successfully by the teacher, thus disputing the teacher's unconscious belief that he is bound to fail with hard-to-manage girls. Finally, the consultant can share incidents with the teacher (stories or parables) that illustrate other teachers gaining control over difficult situations, doing well at work despite stressful home environments, overcoming certain behavioral blocks, and so on.

Caplan (1970) viewed parables as a way to tell consultees important information without directly confronting them concerning their own behaviors. Caplan viewed direct confrontation as unacceptable because such confrontation might arouse unconscious material that would require therapeutic support.

Evaluation Issues. Mental health consultation is successful when consultees seek out the consultant for information and support, feel more self-confident and skillful in their work, and use problem-solving approaches with new problems. Clients' situations should also improve due to the work of a mental health consultant. Client change may come a while after consultee change, however, so early evaluation strategies may focus on consultee attitudes and behaviors more than on clients (see Fuchs & Fuchs, 1989, for an analogous situation using behavioral consultation). After a consultant has worked in an organization for two or three years, client-focused evaluation is an important priority.

Behavioral Consultation

Like mental health consultation, behavioral consultation is a problem-solving framework aimed at improving the performance of both consultees and clients. Unlike mental health consultation, however, behavioral consultation is based on social learning theory and, therefore, considers overt behaviors (skills, knowledge) to be more influential in predicting a consultee's success than are unconscious themes (Bergan, 1977; Bergan & Kratochwill, 1990).

Aspects of behavioral consultation are more familiar to many consultants than mental health consultation. Whatever the espoused theory of most consultants, the majority work to define problems, isolate those environmental variables prompting or supporting target problems, and devise environmental manipulations to reduce the probability of the problem behavior continuing. That is, most consultants tend to be case centered or client centered and not devote too much attention to subtle aspects of consultee adjustment.

Behavioral consultation has been most clearly described with applications in school settings. The approach would be useful in many settings, however.

Entry. Behavioral consultants can tell organizations exactly what they do, provide supportive research evidence, and even delimit the kinds of problems susceptible to their interventions. In contrast to mental health consultation, behavioral practitioners often have specific information on how resistant to change various problems may be, and how long it takes them to impart necessary information to consultees.

Although this sounds ideal, there are entry problems (Piersel & Gutkin, 1983). The major problem has been some resistance to behavior modification. The resistance has arisen because (a) some behavioral consultants were so enthusiastic about their techniques that they failed to be respectful of consultees' existing styles; (b) behavioral consultants have not examined the relationship dimensions of their work with consultees until recently (e.g., Witt & Martens, 1988) and so suggested changes disruptive to consultees; (c) some consultees object to what they understand as a reductionistic understanding of human nature informing behavioral techniques; and (d) many consultees think they already know about behaviorism and that it does not work with their clients.

Social learning theory strategies are effective with many problems, but consultants are well advised to find out if behavioral jargon is acceptable in their organizations. If not, language should be modified accordingly. Behavioral strategies can be described without resorting to jargon. For example, chaining, generalization, modeling, and fixed interval sched les transform to teaching one subskill after another, transferring skills lear ied in one situation to another, showing clients how to do something rather than just telling them to do something, and rewarding clients after a consistent period of time.

Entry is also facilitated if the consultant's early cases do not demand large changes on the part of consultees. For example, asking teachers to implement complex behavioral programs in their classrooms may be unrealistic. Even if teachers try to comply, they are likely to feel so burned out by the endeavor that they may never seek consultation again. In chapter 5 of this book, treatment acceptability considerations are explored that may be important for consultants to consider when suggesting interventions, from any theoretical perspectives.

Targets. Although behavioral consultants work with consultees, they have tended to do so only in an instrumental way. That is, the consultant teaches the consultee a new way of responding to a client's appropriate and inappropriate behaviors. The consultant wants the consultee to behave differently to get the client's behavior under control. Behavioral consultants do not diagnose subtle consultee dynamics, but take a straightforward, information-sharing approach.

There is nothing inherent in social learning theory limiting its use to individual cases, but the practice of behavioral consultation has consisted mainly of interventions with individuals or small groups of clients. In contrast to mental health consultation, there is limited literature concerning relationship issues between the consultant and consultee (Witt & Martens, 1988; Witt, Martens, & Elliott, 1984).

Strategies. The techniques involved in behavioral consultation are diverse but are based on the assumption that environmental manipulations will change behavior. The behavioral model is used extensively in elementary schools and in other environments that are mainly under the control of the caretakers (e.g., prisons, in-patient units, and partial hospitalization units).

Numerous strategies are available to behavioral consultants. The array of social learning and cognitive-behavioral approaches is well represented in journals and looks at simple and sophisticated levels of explanation (e.g., Hughes & Hall, 1989). Consultants must have a thorough understanding of learning principles, recent research evidence, and contexts that make certain interventions more and less acceptable to consultees (Elliott, Witt, Galvin, & Peterson, 1984; Kazdin, 1981; Witt et al., 1984). Most behaviorists now allow for the importance of certain cognitive variables and so might suggest skill acquisition programs like Goldstein's (1981) that rely on learning principles, role-play, feedback, and homework assignments.

Beyond knowing what to say, consultants must know how to talk with consultees. Bergan and his associates (Bergan & Kratochwill, 1990; Bergan & Neumann, 1980; Bergan & Tombari, 1976; Tombari & Bergan, 1978) devoted considerable research energy to identifying effective consultation interview formats and verbal strategies. They suggested viewing behavioral consultation as occurring over four stages or interviews: problem identification, problem analysis, intervention, and evaluation or follow-up.

A mutual understanding of a problem stated in concrete, observable behaviors is critical to the success of behavioral consultation. The problem should be analyzed in terms of its frequency, duration, context, deviation from behavioral norms, and what resources are available to work on the behavior. Consultants help consultees design ways of collecting data about problems, set priorities about targets, and suggest strategies known to be effective in reducing or accelerating certain behaviors. Finally, behavioral consultants value collecting follow-up data concerning the effectiveness of their programs.

Evaluation. Behavioral consultation is the easiest of the consultation approaches to evaluate. Because the process begins with a careful problem definition and specific goal setting, the evaluation plan is simply an extension of the initial data-collecting activity. Client data should be collected by the consultee. The importance of a feasible data collection system cannot be overstated. Consultees have limited time in which to collect data and may, understandably, not value the activity as much as the consultant does. Any collaborative efforts at data collection are probably good ideas. For example, the consultant might collect some of the data, the client could self-monitor, or an aide or volunteer could be enlisted to assist the consultee.

Evaluation results are useful in modifying or abandoning plans and helpful in advertising consultation services to other consultees in an organization. Nothing is more persuasive than evidence that change is possible. Behavioral consultation has shown consistently positive outcomes when implemented correctly (Sibley, 1986); however, often the model is not well implemented. Consultants are known to avoid data collection at baseline and evaluation phases, as well as to provide insufficient support to consultees regarding treatment integrity (Reschly, 1988; Witt, 1986).

Process Consultation

The theoretical roots of the process consultation model lie in social psychology. It is a problem-solving approach that seeks to make people more aware of the interpersonal transactions that are continually affecting their work productivity and morale.

Process consultation is employed frequently in organization development (OD) efforts. Organization development is a collaborative program between consultant and consultees to enhance organizational functioning through improved use of organizational data. It is a program (usually a series of events) aimed at creating renewed and renewing systems that optimally utilize the talent of participants (employees, managers, etc.) while maintaining humane, growth-enhancing environments.

Because the work of most organizations is done in small groups, process consultants concentrate on helping members of the group to see interactional patterns that are interfering with task accomplishment. Such patterns might include poor agenda setting, inconsistent decision-making styles, hidden personal agendas, inappropriately high levels of competition, scapegoating one member or another group, or poor leadership skills on the part of the chief administrator.

Process consultants might also examine the system for structural or procedural problems. Although consultants are not always content experts about an organization's products, they use such techniques as agenda setting, goal setting, role clarification, survey data feedback, confrontation meetings, administrative coaching, and process analysis of meetings to improve how things are done in an organization.

Process consultants make people more aware of the interpersonal process events in their environments and how these events affect their work (Schein, 1969, 1990).

Many consultees tend to be content oriented and not immediately receptive to process consultants. This is ironic, because most complex work is a combination of process and product considerations. Process consultants, like mental health consultants, can find it difficult to describe exactly what their contributions to an organization will be.

In recent years, however, a focus on process has become more common in many organizations. For example, teachers' multiple team memberships have created the need for skills in leading groups, setting agendas, caring for the social and emotional needs of a group, problem solving, conflict management, feedback, communication, decision making, and so on (Conoley, 1989; Norris, Burke, & Speer, 1990). Special education teachers must be especially skilled in group process so they can facilitate placement committee meetings, manage parent conferences, and communicate with their colleagues at problem-solving meetings.

The process consultant recognizes overt and covert events at workgroup meetings and understands the effects these events have on productivity and morale. In schools, the consultant is interested in improving the interpersonal skills used among the adults as well as analyzing classrooms for process events. A process consultant would, for example, be concerned about friendship patterns in a classroom, the emergence of leadership among the students, the existence of a scapegoated minority group of students (ethnic, social class, academic, etc.), the level of cooperation versus competition characterizing a classroom, and a teacher's abilities to create a task-oriented, instructional environment for children.

In contrast to mental health consultants, process consultants are not concerned about unconscious dynamics among staff members. Unlike behavioral consultants, the process consultant usually targets consultee skills at handling organizational problems instead of focusing on clients' behaviors per se. The theory guiding this work stems from research on small groups, organizational effectiveness, and social psychology (see Conoley & Gutkin, 1986b).

Entry. Process consultation is best introduced in an organization with strong support from the chief executive. Although administrator sanction is important before offering any consultation, process consultation requires special attention. Some of the roles a process consultant might play are those occupied by the administrator. It is important that the leader understands the short- and long-term goals of interventions and is supportive of the consultant's work.

For example, a resource teacher interested in process consultation could target group dynamics at placement meetings. This consultant might believe that increased problem-solving interactions would improve the services offered to children. If the building principal chairs the placement meeting, he or she must approve the work of the consultant. Without prior approval, the consultant could be perceived as trying to assume the chair's prerogatives. Although some principals (and administrators from many fields) are delighted to share power and roles, others perceive sharing as a threat.

All members of an organization should be told of the possibilities available through a focus on group information and process. Often, process consultants begin their services via a large group meeting on communicating with peers, creating positive meeting climates, or eliminating roadblocks to effective problem solving. In addition to presentations, a process consultant might introduce services through a needs-analysis project. For example, with principal approval, the special education consultant could survey teachers to discover teachers' perceptions of gaps in services for children, teacher preferences for in-service training concerning special needs children, or teachers' views on aspects of organizational functioning that support or inhibit teaching special education children.

Following the collection of such information, the process consultant initiates feedback and problem-solving sessions with teachers to identify teacher priorities and make plans to meet their stated needs. This process of organizational diagnosis and action planning is critical to the process consultation model. The ultimate goal of the process consultant is to facilitate ongoing organizational analysis and renewal.

Target. Process consultants focus their work on the interactions among people in work groups. They try to improve the way problems are solved, decisions are made, work is coordinated, and innovation is incorporated.

To do so, the consultant may engage in some individual coaching of team leaders or other administrators, but the actual targets are those processes that occur in every human system; for example, emergent leadership, time keeping, information or opinion giving and seeking, communication patterns, offering help, blocking actions, tension releasing, encouraging, clarifying, feedback, compromising, and so on. The process consultant wants to improve both the productivity of a work group (e.g., faculty, classroom, team) and the morale of the group.

Strategies. To accomplish their goals, process consultants involve themselves in data-gathering activities (e.g., surveys, interviews, observation), data feedback activities, simulations, and occasional didactic inputs. The didactics are aimed at giving consultees skills in observing, analyzing, and changing their own processes.

For example, once organizational members understand what group processes are and the effects of these, work-group members can examine their own processes after they have finished a task. The group members reflect on how they used time, how decisions were made, and whether everyone felt involved, invested, and valued. The group members can then make plans for the improvement or maintenance of their skill levels. Early attempts at this may require consultant support, but the goal would be to make such observations a regular part of most meetings.

Evaluation. Process consultation is evaluated by requesting feedback from group members on their increased knowledge and use of group skills and their perceptions of how well tasks are accomplished and about the quality of their work lives. In addition, objective measures of productivity and organizational morale can be examined. Process consultants should be aware that consultees are often uncomfortable in discussing group process or receiving and giving feedback. This discomfort must be treated with respect. Feedback must be given carefully, confidential information guarded, and people's readiness to engage with one another diagnosed continuously.

A UNIFYING PERSPECTIVE

Consultation is probably best conceptualized as drawing from each of the aforementioned models, creating an ecological model of consultation. In essence, the most successful consultants are expert in knowing about the internal motivational states of their colleagues (mental health consultation), the environmental conditions that promote or inhibit positive behaviors and accomplishments (behavioral consultation), and optimal ways of getting along with others and helping others to get along with each other (process consultation).

Proponents of the ecological orientation take the position that behavior is determined by the interaction of individual and environmental characteristics. Although all major approaches to understanding human behavior cite internal and external forces as operating together to produce behavior, they differ significantly in emphasis.

For example, both psychodynamic and biophysical models are concerned for the most part with the definition and understanding of internal forces. Psychodynamic theorists focus primarily on needs and drives and on the investigation of patterns of behavior that occur at various stages of development. Biophysical theorists, on the other hand, emphasize physiological conditions that may lead to certain typical behavior patterns.

Behavioral and sociological models are concerned mainly with external forces. The behavior theorist tries to understand stimulus–response patterns and the reinforcing and punishing conditions in the environment that produce particular sequences of behaviors. This is a functional analysis of behavior. Sociologists are more concerned with the broader environment, including institutions, communities, culture, and society, in their efforts to understand conditions that produce individual and group behavior.

Ecological theory maintains an equal concern for internal and external forces when attempting to understand human behavior. Ecologists assume there is a unique pattern of explanatory forces for each individual case under scrutiny. Gordon (1982), describing ecological theory, noted the following:

> While the individual is being examined, the model simultaneously permits the worker to study the environment, seeking beneficial changes in the total structure, redefining the goals, and exploring the ability of the client to survive in that state, as well as the potential of both for changed existence in improved states. (p. 110)

Ecologists examine ecosystems rather than individuals. Ecosystems are composed of all the interacting systems of living things and their nonliving surroundings. Ecosystems have histories and internal development that make each unique and constantly changing. When a child appears normal, ecologists see the ecosystem as congruent or balanced. On the other hand, when such congruence does not exist, the child is likely to be considered deviant (i.e., out of harmony with social norms) or incompetent (i.e., unable to perform purposefully in the unchanged setting). When this is the case, ecologists say the system is not balanced, that particular elements are in conflict with one another. Such conflicts are termed *points of discordance,* that is, specific places where there is a failure to match between the child and his or her ecosystem.

The major assumptions of the ecological model applied to consultation relationships serve as key concepts in developing interventions.

1. *Each person is an inseparable part of a small social system.* Every individual lives in a context that is both unique and critical to our understanding of the person and our intervention efforts.

2. *Disturbance is viewed not as a disease located within the body (or mind) of a person but, rather, as discordance in the system.* Contrary to psychodynamic or biophysical models in which the disease defined the client, from the ecological position a troubled youngster or situation represents a troubled system (Apter, 1982). For example, environments may elicit disturbing behaviors and then identify and label such behaviors as symptoms of emotional disturbance or behavior disorder. Which behaviors get labeled depend on the time, place, and culture in which they are emitted and on the tolerance of those who observe them (Rhodes, 1967; Swap, Prieto, & Harth, 1982).

3. *Discordance may be defined as a disparity between an individual's abilities and the demands or expectations of the environment—a failure to match between a person and system.* Some settings are demanding and unresponsive to the individual abilities of clients or consultees. In such environments, individuals may appear incompetent, while in other more nurturing environments the same person will not be identified as deviant. An example may be the so-called 6-hour retarded child—a child labeled as retarded by the school but considered normal in the family and community. Another example are children identified as having specific learning disabilities. These disabilities are rarely noticeable before or after a child has completed formal education (Reschly, 1988).

In sum, the goal of ecologically based consultation is not a particular state of mental health or particular behavior patterns, but rather an increased concordance between the behavior and attitudes of a person and the settings in which he or she resides. These goals are reached not through a new set of techniques or treatments but through a framework of using existing techniques in an ecological manner. The ecological perspective is a useful umbrella to organize a variety of intervention efforts into a purposeful attempt to increase the possibility of system change, the competence of individuals, and the congruence of individuals with their settings.

School-based consultants drawing from ecological understandings of behavior (Apter, 1982; Apter & Conoley, 1984; Conoley & Haynes, in press; Hobbs, 1982) are interested in improving people skills, coordinating the services offered to students and teachers, and helping teachers, parents, and students to hold realistic, yet high, expectations toward one another.

The key task of the consultant is to use theory to inform practice; that is, to be sophisticated about what helps people change their skills, attitudes, behaviors, and expectations (Idol & West, 1987). Great effort and commitment are needed, however, to fulfill the potential contributions of ecologically based consultation.

SUMMARY

Consultation, a voluntary problem-solving relationship between professionals, can be conceptualized from a number of practical and theoretical perspectives. Perhaps the most helpful approach is to consider consultation from an ecological perspective. In this way, the range of techniques, targets, and available worldviews is enhanced. Such flexibility seems warranted if consultants want to be effective with the widest array of organizations, consultees, and clients.

SUGGESTED READINGS

Alpert, J. L. (1989). Change within a profession: Change, future, prevention, and school psychology. *American Psychologist, 40,* 1112–1121.

Babcock, N. L., & Pryzwansky, W. B. (1983). Models of consultation: Preferences of educational professionals at five stages of service. *Journal of School Psychology, 21,* 359–366.

Brown, D., Pryzwansky, W. B., & Schulte, A. C. (1987). *Psychological consultation: Introduction to theory and practice.* Poston: Allyn & Bacon.

Gutkin, T. B., & Curtis, M. J. (1990). School-based consultation: Theory, techniques, and research. In T. B. Gutkin & C. R. Reynolds (Eds.), *Handbook of school psychology* (pp. 577–613). New York: John Wiley & Sons.

Chapter 2
Skills Needed for Consultation

Good consultants have mastered a comprehensive package of skills and attitudes related to interpersonal influence, problem formulation and resolution, ethical behavior, and sensitivity to individual differences among consultees and clients. The skills and attitudes discussed in this chapter combine process and content domains but relate primarily to a consultant's expertise in managing process events in the environment. Specialized content knowledge must also be mastered. Examples of content needs are developed in chapter 3.

RELATIONSHIP-ENHANCING SKILLS

Preferred consultants are friendly, egalitarian, open, skilled in group management, aware of and sympathetic to the situations of consultees, supportive, flexible, efficient, and exhibit good follow-up or follow-through skills and nonthreatening expertise (Bergan & Tombari, 1976; Cutler & McNeil, 1964; Mannino, 1969; Robbins & Spencer, 1968; Schowengerdt, Fine, & Poggio, 1976).

Consultees report valuing positive, supportive consultants as much or more than even knowledgeable but authoritarian experts. An awareness of the personal impact of the consultant and importance of the consultation relationship is basic to all consultation training and practice. Knowing something well does not guarantee you will help others know it. Good consultants, good therapists, and good teachers are experts in content, and in motivating others to learn, change behavior, or conceptualize issues in new ways. Such consultants radiate concern for the people in the relationship, not only for the problem under discussion.

19

Consultants who are experts in listening, giving and receiving feedback, and formulating and resolving problems are well on the way toward mastery of consultation. If these skills are combined with a sensitivity to others in terms of culture, gender, and physical and mental abilities, then all that is necessary in addition is content information useful to a particular consultee faced with a particular dilemma.

Being perfect doesn't hurt! In lieu of perfection, however, acquisition of the skills outlined in the following sections is necessary.

Listening

Hearing precisely what someone has said and helping the speaker feel understood is a basic consultation skill. Good listening is composed of verbal skills and nonverbal habits. The verbal components of good listening skills include acknowledging, reflecting, paraphrasing, summarizing, clarifying, and elaborating.

Acknowledging. Acknowledging refers to words such as *yes, really, wow, right,* and *good.* These words are helpful in encouraging consultees to speak. They also communicate some awareness of the emotional content of the consultee's message.

Reflecting. Reflective listening is the process of repeating back to the consultee his or her words. The repetitions are not, of course, done in a parrot-like fashion. The consultant can choose the words, phrases, or sentences to reflect back to the consultee, to underline the importance of some information or to move the conversation in a particular direction.

Consultee: I'm so frustrated that Doreen runs around all day.
Consultant: Oh, you're feeling frustrated.
                                          or
Consultant: She runs around all day, huh?

The first choice will direct the session toward the consultee's emotional responses to his or her situation; the second will begin the process of behavioral analysis.

Paraphrasing. Paraphrasing is somewhat more complex than reflective listening. It involves substituting synonyms for the consultee's words and saying those interpretations back. In paraphrasing, the consultant can heighten or reduce the power of what is said, slightly change a meaning, or be faithful to the message of the consultee. Such a process is used not to test the vocabulary skills of the consultant, but to cue the consultee to slight variations in his or her message.

Consultant: You seem to be angry at Doreen's activity.

or

Consultant: You're concerned about Doreen's movement.

Paraphrases must be offered tentatively so the consultee can feel free to challenge the consultant's interpretation. Such challenges are often instructive. A consultee may dispute the word *angry*. Many caregivers, for example, do not believe they are supposed to get angry. Such an emotion may seem unprofessional. A consultant can use such an interaction to discuss the indirect effects and costs of suppressed anger. The consultant can do so without disagreeing with the consultee.

Consultee: I'm not angry with her. I don't get angry at children. That's not my job.

Consultant: I may have misunderstood. I know some behaviors do make me angry when I've tried and tried to correct them. I find that my anger is a good barometer of how frustrating a situation is for me.

Consultee: Well, that's certainly true. I've been frustrated by Doreen.

Consultant: The ironic thing is that the more angry I am, the less creative I get in coming up with solutions for my problems. That's when it's good to get somebody else's suggestions.

Consultee: That's probably where I am right this minute with Doreen.

Summarizing. Periodically, a consultant can provide summary statements. These might describe what behavioral antecedents or consequences have been described thus far, or what remedial strategies have been suggested. Skillful summarizing seems to help in making decisions, preserving information, and ending meetings.

A consultee will often be pleased and surprised that a consultant has listened carefully enough to be able to list back most of the conversation's important points.

Consultant: So far, you've told me about Teddy's academic problems, behavior problems, and family problems. You really have a lot of information about this child.

Consultee: And you have a great memory.

Consultant: I think it's a good time to choose a few high-priority issues to work on. What do you think? Should we try to increase his daily work completion or go for a parent conference right away?

Written records of the session can be used. The progress notes shown in Figure 2.1 are an example of written summarization.

Clarifying. Clarification involves asking questions that invite elaboration on previously made points. Consultants should try to understand completely

To (consultee)   Date _____
From (consultant)   We've met with (any other consultees or client)
regarding (client name or problem situation)

We've discussed these concerns:

(Description of the problem)

Possible strategies:

(List top-ranked solutions that have been generated.)

We've tried these strategies: Effective   Not effective

(Note previous attempts and their effectiveness.)

We are working on the following:

(Plans for implementation, contacts to be made,
resources to be found)

Comments:

(What is the next step; when is the next meeting?)

FIGURE 2.1. Example of a form used to record progress notes.

what the consultee has said about a problem. Consultants ask questions
not simply to gain information, but also to give consultees practice in
putting their information together in helpful, problem-solving ways.

Clarifying does not mean rapid-fire questions following from the consultant's agenda. Rather, clarification is a balance between consultant hypotheses and consultee leads.

Consultant: You mentioned that disruptive activity is a problem. When
is it the worst? Is there a pattern in terms of time of day, subject
taught, peer group, teacher, or some other situation that seems to
make the behavior better or worse?

Consultee: I hadn't thought there was any pattern, but I really haven't
tried to notice. The running around is so annoying.

Consultant: Well, there may not be a pattern. If there is one, it's
usually easier to get some improvement.

Consultee: Actually, now that we talk about it, it seems that she's
pretty good in spelling and in reading. Reading is first thing in the
morning; spelling is the next to the last period.

Elaborating. Elaborating involves building on what has already been introduced into a conversation. Often we can begin an elaboration by saying,

"Taking off from what you've said . . ." or "I'm thinking about what you suggested. Would this fit as part of that plan?"

Elaborating has a number of benefits in a problem-solving sequence. First, it allows for more complex and comprehensive plans to be formulated. Second, it makes people feel invested in the process, because their ideas have been heard, valued, and used. It is critical, of course, to give credit to others when building on their ideas. Do not commit the classic error of introducing as your own a thought that was actually first mentioned by the consultee. Whenever possible, consultees should be given primary credit for having all the best ideas.

Elaboration is helpful because it highlights the coordinate nature of the plans being considered. By linking consultant suggestions to consultee verbalizations, the final product is clearly a joint venture.

Consultee: I think the only way to handle this problem is by getting her out of the classroom. She's just too distractable to be with 22 other children.

Consultant: The idea of excluding her sometimes or having some private place for her to go is really an interesting one. Your school has a Quiet Room, doesn't it?

Nonverbal Skills

The best consultants maintain comfortable levels of eye contact (but don't stare); orient their bodies toward the consultee so the consultee knows the consultant is attentive (lean forward a little in your chair toward the consultee); avoid nervous habits or excessive note taking; and nod, smile, or make acknowledging sounds (mmm, uh-huh) to encourage the consultee to continue. The consultant wants to project calm concern, assurance (but not too much reassurance; remember, a little anxiety is good for performance), and intense interest in and respect for the consultee.

Humans tend to accomplish a lot of their communication nonverbally. Facial expressions, gait, hand movements, and general demeanor are all factors that enter into a consultee's judgment about a consultant. Feedback from others is the only way we learn what our nonverbals are communicating.

Feedback

Feedback is often misunderstood as implying only negative information. In fact, feedback is any information that can be shared with another that informs that person about the effects of his or her behavior on us. The information is shared as a way to help another person consider a behavior change—for example, doing more or less of some behavior.

Feedback is not simply "what I saw you do and my evaluation of it." Rather, it is a process that should be initiated among people who are in a relationship and who are not demanding a behavior change but are offering information that might facilitate one.

Feedback skills are critical in consultation. The consultant maintains a nonjudgmental attitude toward consultees but must be skilled in sharing important information with them. Consultants must also seek and respond nondefensively to feedback from the consultee. Effective giving and receiving of feedback models skills for the consultee as well as increases the impact of the services provided by the consultant.

Giving Feedback. In assessing feedback skills, the following guidelines are helpful:

1. Make a decision regarding the usefulness or potential influence of your feedback to the consultee. Be sure you are not trying to punish the consultee.
2. Describe what you have observed the consultee do in terms that are not evaluative, demeaning, or judgmental. Describe the way the behavior has affected you.
3. State the feedback in a somewhat tentative way so the consultee feels free to probe for more information. Also, the consultee should not feel pressured because you, as consultant, tell him or her to change.
4. Focus feedback on aspects of the consultee that can be changed. For example, telling someone that his or her African heritage makes you uncomfortable cannot facilitate change in the ethnicity of the consultee. Such a statement says more about you than about the consultee.
5. Timing is important. Optimally, give feedback when it is asked for; when the person seems able to hear (i.e., is not preoccupied with something else), when the person is not overwhelmed with feedback from others, and as close to the occurrence of the target behavior as possible. Do not give feedback because you have had enough or are angry or punitive.
6. Check the consultee's understanding of feedback by asking him or her to repeat what you have said.

Consultant: For the 10 minutes I observed in your class I noticed you use four different techniques to help Collin begin his work. You reminded him, you stood by him, you asked another student to assist him, and you praised him when you saw that he had begun. Those are the ones I saw; did I miss any?

This feedback is better than saying, "You did great," because it gives the receiver specific information about his or her behavior.

What if you've observed an unsuccessful situation and are asked to provide feedback?

Consultant: I saw Molly out of her seat and not responsive to your attempt to get her to work. What I saw was that you relied on verbal reprimand. Seeing Molly's reaction makes me think that we should work together to generate some other activities or strategies. I may be off base, but I also sensed that you were pretty frustrated by the encounters. Your face seemed tight and tired.

Consultants often see direct feedback (especially negative feedback) as a last resort. School consultants tend to provide classroom management procedures to consultees as a first strategy. They do not focus on the teacher as implementor, but rather act as if a good idea will be implemented. Sometimes that happens. An already skilled, flexible teacher takes a new idea and uses it effectively. When implementation does not occur, however, the consultant is placed in the position of coming up with more and better ideas or carefully examining the implementation variables impeding the new program.

When observation reveals that the teacher's implementation is incorrect and/or the teacher is emitting many counterproductive behaviors, the consultant can feel pressed to give the teacher feedback likely to be experienced as negative. Direct or indirect confrontation may be necessary. The following is an example of direct confrontation:

Consultant: Your frequent use of sarcastic statements with the children makes me feel somewhat intimidated. Do you suppose the children could experience those statements in this way?

or

Consultant: I felt you were anxious about disciplining the class because of the number of times you said you were sorry about telling them what to do. Do you feel somewhat uneasy about controlling the class?

The following is an example of indirect confrontation:

Consultant: This child does not qualify for out-of-classroom special service. How can I help you cope better with the situation in the classroom?

or

Consultant: The home situation is terrible, but all we can control are these 6 hours—probably the best, most consistent 6 hours of this child's day. How can we structure a predictable context for Tommy?

The difference between the direct and indirect feedback confrontations is the focus; that is, either on the person or on the issue: "You are making sarcastic statements" or "You seem anxious" versus "Special class placement is impossible" or "The home may be difficult to modify." Using direct confrontation involves identifying the consultee as the target of the feedback. Indirect confrontation involves conceptualizing the problem as the issue it represents and placing the problem on the issue.

Consultant: I have not observed you trying the techniques we discussed to increase Tonya's time on task. I'm wondering if you are feeling unable to keep her in your class or are hoping that she will be moved?

versus

Consultant: I didn't notice you trying the techniques we discussed to increase Tonya's time on task. This suggests to me the ideas we developed don't seem to fit as well as I'd hoped. What have you experienced?

The first verbalization is a direct question about a teacher's professionalism that may threaten the consultation relationship. The second assumes that the problem is with the plan, not with the consultee. If possible, the second type may be better to use than the first.

This extended discussion of confrontive feedback does not mean that feedback is such a difficult skill that it is a last resort. At the beginning stages of problem identification and analysis (Bergan & Kratochwill, 1990; Bergan & Tombari, 1976), the consultant should be providing the consultee with feedback about how his or her classroom context and style match potential strategies.

During a classroom observation, for example, the consultant can develop feedback about the target children and the teacher. This immediate connection between strategy and strategist opens the way for continuous feedback rather than desperate final attempts. The following example illustrates this point.

In a second-grade classroom, Mrs. Smith, a 28-year teaching veteran, experienced difficulty with classroom management. Two boys were focal, but the teacher described the whole class as being somewhat out of control. The consultant observed that the teacher jumped from disruption to disruption in the classroom and made many irrelevant verbal statements, but did make use of some group and individual positive statements. The teacher was willing to begin new strategies but would, after a day or so, lose confidence that they would work and so discontinue use.

The consultant worked on a plan involving the presentation of stars or stickers to well-behaved children. Although somewhat successful (the teacher and principal commented on a moderate class improvement), the strategy was inconsistently applied because of the teacher's habit of responding primarily to disruptive children.

The consultant's first impulse was to give the teacher feedback on her poor plan implementation. A further analysis of the problem situation suggested, however, that a plan involving only positive attention did not fit the teacher's style. The fact that it was working at all was a credit to the strength of positive consequences.

The consultant and teacher worked out another plan involving the two target boys and the classroom. Some of the plan components included (a) positive individual attention to the target children contingent on completion of assignments (they were already doing some work); (b) classroom rules worked on, one per day, until five or six had been formulated and learned by the children; (c) a daily surprise activity (list suggested by the teacher) for well-behaved children; and (d) an hour off per month to observe the class as the principal took over.

This case highlights an important way to incorporate feedback and plan implementation. When the second plan was worked out, each step was paired with observable teacher behavior. During implementation, teacher feedback was not risky, because the teacher's teaching style had already been discussed and incorporated into the intervention.

Consultant: Here's something I already see you do. You lean down and compliment Matt quietly when you see him working. Did you realize that you did that twice yesterday morning, and he was on task for 15 minutes following each time you did it?

Consultee: No, I didn't. Of course, you know Matt. He has his good and bad days. One time when I leaned down to talk with him, he turned so fast that he bumped my face. Now he was nice about that. He said, "Did I hurt you? I'm sorry."

Consultant: So you are already aware of it in some ways—how much impact you have on him sometimes. I wonder if you could do more of what you're already doing to Kent and Matt in terms of quiet positive statements. I'll keep a log of the results.

Consultee: If you think so. Of course, you know I have some weak ones in here—some like I've had every year, but some others that are really something.

Consultant: You have a lot of experience. I bet you've developed lots of stuff for the kids to do in terms of activities over the past years. I really admire your willingness to try new things.

Consultee: Well, you have to be willing to change. Kids are different. Look at this [points to file]. This is my collection of 28 years' worth of activities.

Consultant: What a resource! Would you mind if I looked at that stuff? I'm sure it would give me ideas for other teachers.

The consultant began building on teacher strengths instead of designing plans that did not match her existing skills. Each component was tied to an openly discussed teacher propensity.

Receiving Feedback. It is almost impossible (and undesirable) to avoid getting feedback. In fact, Rae-Grant (1972) mentions avoiding feedback as one way to be a failure as a consultant. Formal evaluation instruments for providing feedback to the consultant are discussed in chapter 6. Often, however, positive and negative feedback come spontaneously.

Consultants must be able to accept gracefully what is offered. Such grace is good modeling and encourages the flow of valid information (Argyris, 1971). Ideally, consultants should elicit feedback routinely and respond nondefensively. The following are some basic guidelines to consider when receiving feedback.

1. Develop a relaxation response (e.g., deep breathing or muscle relaxation) to use when you become aware that feedback is imminent.
2. Listen closely to everything the consultee is saying. Do not begin to formulate a response until the entire message has been delivered.
3. Try to catch the essence of the feelings the consultee is sharing.
4. Before speaking, get in touch with your own feelings. Give your feelings a name.
5. Repeat what you've heard. Ask for clarification, if necessary. In a group, check to see if others see you in a similar way.
6. Remember, you have no way to control the way others see you. You are completely responsible only for your own behavior. Perhaps you will decide to change a behavior that someone finds unfavorable. You cannot be sure, however, that the person's feelings about you will change if you do so.
7. Unless there is a content misunderstanding between you and the feedback giver, do not give reasons why you have behaved the way you did.

Consultee: Those suggestions you gave me had no effect on Jose. He didn't finish a single problem!

Consultant: Thanks for letting me know there's a concern. When can we spend a few minutes clarifying the problem so that I can be more helpful?

The consultee is not asking you to change, but is telling you how behavior X (e.g., your recent advice) affects the target person. The information is valuable even if you didn't mean to do X or you thought the person asked for X, and so on.

Consultee: You are wonderful. I really appreciate your suggestions and support.

Consultant: Thank you. Your openness has made me feel successful about our work.

or

Consultee: I had the whole class waiting for you. Where were you?

Consultant: I am sorry you were inconvenienced. Which day are we talking about?

Consultee: Wednesday.

Consultant: Thank you for mentioning this to me. I have to find out why my telephone messages are not being passed on. I called the office Wednesday with a message to you, but I guess I needed to be more explicit that you needed to know that I was sick with the flu.

Consultee: I didn't know you had the flu! We waited only a few minutes before I figured you weren't coming.

PROBLEM FORMULATION AND RESOLUTION

Skills highlighted in the previous sections will contribute to effective problem solving. In addition, it is helpful to have a plan or steps to follow when faced with a troubling issue. The following discussion illustrates a typical problem-solving sequence. The sequence deserves some elaboration because there are special pitfalls at each step.

Some research in consultation (Bergan & Tombari, 1975) suggests that problem formulation or problem identification is the most important part of problem solving. This may seem obvious—you cannot solve a problem before you know what it is. In practice, however, there is a tendency for consultants and consultees to jump to generating solutions before they have a clear, mutually understood problem definition.

Before determining how to deal with a problem, the consultant and consultee should determine what the problem includes. Bergan and Tombari (1975) suggested an analysis phase during which the environment the problem occurs in is investigated, the skills and talents of the people involved are discussed, the antecedents and consequences of the troublesome event are specified, and data from others in the child's environment, past and present, are collected. In this way, the problem and its context are completely understood before moving toward brainstorming solutions.

A consultant will want to elicit information from the consultee about the characteristics of the setting in which the behaviors occur (e.g., small or large group, particular tasks being done), about individual characteristics of the client (e.g., age, learning aptitudes or disabilities), and about the history of previous remediation attempts. The problem definition should include the current behavior of the client and the desired outcomes. In this way, a discrepancy between the current state and desired state of affairs can be articulated. The establishment of a criterion for success is invaluable for future evaluation. Knowledge of what a consultee would accept as successful is also important.

If the consultee has a realistic projection of what improvement can be expected from a client, the consultant knows that a case-centered approach is appropriate. If, however, the consultee's goals are inappropriate for the age, readiness, or skill level of the client, the consultant must use a consultee-centered approach.

The problem identification phase may be the most important component to successful problem resolution. Witt and Elliott (1983) identified nine components of an appropriate initial interview with a consultee: (a) explanation of the need to define the problem; (b) identification and selection of a target behavior for change; (c) identification of problem frequency, duration, and intensity; (d) identification of the conditions under which the behavior of concern occurs; (e) identification of the required level of performance; (f) identification of the client's strengths; (g) identification of behavioral assessment procedures; (h) identification of consultee effectiveness; and (i) summarization and establishment of time frame for future contacts with consultant.

As difficult as it is to accomplish all of the aforementioned components, there are additional challenges. Consultants must keep in mind that consultee problems have resisted the consultee's efforts at remediation. The consultee has constructed a meaning related to the problematic situation that is of primary importance. That is, the consultee's construction of the problem is the consultation problem. Consultants should be sophisticated in understanding how people create their realities and should not imagine that they are searching outside of the consultee for the problem.

Plan Generation

Beginning consultants are often fearful that they will not make good suggestions. Once a problem is clearly defined, however, brainstorming (i.e., consultee and consultant generate ideas without evaluation) can be used to generate high-quality ideas. Even if brainstorming does not result in the needed solutions, the process sets the tone for acceptance and divergent thinking. Consultants or consultees can search the literature or ask others for advice in addition to brainstorming.

When choosing among the solutions generated, it is helpful to make the criteria for choice explicit. For example, feasible (i.e., easy to implement) solutions are preferable to grandiose, disruptive solutions. Solutions that can be implemented with minimal guidance from a consultant are preferable to ones that are dependent on consultant involvement. Solutions that build on existing structures or habits are preferable to ones that entail new learning of procedural changes. Early in the consultation relationship the consultant may not have too much credibility and, therefore, not inspire the consultee to make such changes.

Finally, whatever solution is chosen, the choice should sound tentative. Even if the consultant is positive this is *the answer,* such enthusiasm should not be communicated to the consultee. Consultants can help consultees realize that many different approaches may have to be tried before improvement is apparent. Consultees must also realize that nothing works forever. They must understand, for example, that changing environmental contingencies may not cure a problem. The problem might reappear when it is again sustained by environmental rewards and punishments.

The interaction of the individual and his or her context is a difficult concept to transmit. Most of us regard problem behavior as residing within a person. We fail to see the complexity of forces that sustain or inhibit a particular behavior. Lewin (1951) and others (Apter, 1982; Apter & Conoley, 1984; Conoley & Haynes, in press; Rhodes & Tracy, 1972) formulated ecological theories that should be examined before beginning the problem-solving process.

When developing the plan of action, be as specific as possible, especially about roles and time lines. Often, consultees leave a consultation session believing that the consultant will accomplish most of the plan and do it immediately. Being clear avoids feelings of disappointment later in the relationship. If the plan seems too cumbersome or demanding for the consultee to manage alone, it probably is not a good plan.

Implementation

During implementation, consultants should keep in touch with consultees. This is true even if the consultant has no active part in plan implementation. Consultees may need clarification of a point or may simply need reassurance (Fuchs & Fuchs, 1989; Tyler & Fine, 1974; White & Fine, 1976). Consultees prefer intensive involvement with the consultant while they are carrying out jointly developed suggestions. The plan will be implemented with greater success if such contact is maintained.

Treatment integrity or procedural validity is an important issue. Consultants cannot assume that consultees will make complex behavioral changes without cuing, monitoring, and reinforcement. Good consultation requires multiple contacts with consultees during implementation phases.

Plan Evaluation

Evaluation is an important, yet often neglected, part of the problem-resolution sequence. Sometimes the consultant and consultee decide the plan is not working but do not specify whether the plan needs to be changed, abandoned, or tried for a longer period. More often, a strategy is tried, does not seem effective, and is abandoned with no follow-up analysis. This practice reduces the amount of new information available to both the consultant and the consultee for use with current and future problems.

The consultant must create the expectation that many strategies may have to be attempted and that the failure of one does not mean that consultation or attempts to improve the situation should be terminated. Recycling through the problem-solving process is the optimal strategy when success has eluded the consultee on the first (or 10th) attempt. Keeping the consultee's enthusiasm for such refinement is not a trivial problem.

Other Variables Affecting Problem Solving

Gutkin and his associates (e.g., Cleven & Gutkin, 1988) found problem solving to be improved if consultants make the problem-solving sequence known to consultees as their conversations unfold. Gutkin called this a "process-overt" strategy.

Consultant: First, we should be clear that we both understand what
    we're working on. Once we both really understand what you are
    experiencing, we can think of some solutions.

The status of the consultant can also affect a consultee's evaluation of and receptivity to consultant suggestions. Although consultees prefer egalitarian consultants, they nonetheless are influenced most effectively by authoritative experts. Consultants can gain status both through their expertise and through their skillful interaction with consultees (French & Raven, 1959; Martin, 1983).

Openness to the Unlikely

There is another dimension to problem solving that is difficult to define or sequence. This is problem solving that requires skills in the reformulation of problem statements and seemingly incongruous, illogical solution generation.

Watzlawick, Weakland, and Fisch (1974) described this process as second-order change. They drew a distinction between second-order change (i.e., real change or innovation) and first-order change (i.e., simply more of the same).

One advantage of adopting an ecological model of consultation is that it provides various vantage points from which to examine a problem. Flexibility is a consultative advantage because it facilitates the possibility of second-order change formulations. Real change (i.e., change that makes a difference) usually depends on the ability to see a problem from an entirely new perspective. This new perspective often indicates that the solutions currently implemented are the real problems.

For example, a principal who complains about the dishonesty of the staff may put locks on all the phones during lunch hours and after work. The principal may also implement an elaborate surveillance system to monitor arrivals, departures, sick days, and so on. The staff may respond with increased attempts to beat the system and decreased morale and cohesiveness. A second-order change strategy might be to abandon all monitoring procedures (e.g., locks, time clocks) that suggest that the teachers are untrustworthy. A principal may find such advice inconceivable. The problem may not be unmotivated staff but an incorrectly motivated staff. The apparent problems with a staff may not come from inside the individual worker, but from the climate of distrust that the principal projects.

A mastery of ecological theory may help a consultant reconceptualize a problem a number of times until a helpful problem formulation is attained. This skill, although fairly simple to describe, is difficult to master. All of us tend to get stuck in our ways of seeing the world.

Consultant: We've been struggling with this problem of improving Melba's grades by providing her with academic resource help. Nothing's happening. I wonder if we should be looking at something else.

Consultee: She's the one who'll have to change. No one can make her do the work.

Consultant: Well, you're right, of course, that she's at the center of this problem. I seem to remember that she's got a real strained relationship with her stepfather. I wonder if there's an opening. If the stepfather was more influential with her, perhaps Melba would be more likely to apply herself to school work. Right now, it seems that she just doesn't care one way or the other.

Consultee: Well, her mother said that she wished Melba and the stepfather could get along better. Apparently, it's a big problem around the house.

Consultant: Let's arrange for a meeting. If Melba began wanting to please her stepfather, then she might be a bit more compliant at school.

In addition, the consultant must master the process of reframing. This involves casting a problem in a new light, emphasizing the positive aspects of the problem over its negative consequences, and highlighting what adaptive purposes the problem serves.

For example, a child's constant talking to the teacher or clinging behavior can be seen as evidence of the child's positive attachment to the teacher, rather than merely as an annoying habit. By emphasizing attachment over irritation, the consultant can show the teacher how influential he or she can be in a child's life.

The same behavior could be conceptualized as a normal developmental process necessary for the subsequent appearance of independence. In a similar manner, consultants may be able to point out how a child's misbehavior is symptomatic of physical problems not under the immediate volition of the child.

For example, one client had been described as exhibiting annoying and somewhat bizarre self-stimulating behaviors in the class (e.g., noise making, rocking, hand clapping, head rolling) by a teacher who had cajoled, rewarded, and finally spanked the child. The child was at or above grade level in work but did not hand in all assignments. Careful observation and interviewing led the consultant to discover that the child was experiencing petit mal seizures. This new understanding of the behaviors led to an immediate improvement in the strained teacher-child relationship. The improvement significantly preceded the medical alleviation of the child's symptoms.

Obviously, the problem was not the actual behaviors but the teacher's perception of the child as a willfully disobedient student. The behaviors had always been of relatively low frequency and duration and went mainly unnoticed by the rest of the class (see Witt & Martens, 1988, for a fascinating discussion of this phenomenon).

PERSONAL AND GROUP
PROCESS SKILLS

Although there are differences between consultation and counseling (Henning-Stout & Conoley, 1987; McCready, 1985), consultants must possess all the basic and advanced counseling skills. High-quality implementation of skills, however, depends on important personal qualities.

Consultants must be able to say positive, supportive statements to others. A consultee's self-efficacy must be enhanced if behavior change is to be attempted (Bandura, 1986). Consultants' propensity to be positive is directly related to their skills in staying accepting of consultees and clients. Believing that everyone is doing the best they can under current situations is a way to remain accepting. Sometimes what people are able to accomplish is dismally inadequate, but most are trying.

Being congruent (i.e., consultant's feelings and behaviors are well integrated; consultants can speak and behave in ways that match a consultee's mood or concerns) with self and consultees is a basis of trust in the consultation relationship. Consultees should discover that consultants are predictable (i.e., their actions match their words) and that they stay sensitive to consultees' emotional states.

Empathy—the ability to understand another's position—is requisite for consultation. The best consultants know and feel consultees' dilemmas. They are able to maintain a helpful distance from problems (i.e., they do not get so involved that they lose perspective or stay so distant that they miss the crucial nuances of the problem). Note the similarity between being perceptive and being empathic. Both imply an understanding of the consultee. Empathy is concerned with emotional sensitivity, while perceptiveness may be associated with an expert, intuitive content grasp of what a consultee is presenting. The perceptive consultant sees links among bits of information and grasps patterns that are unnoticed by consultees.

Consultants should be self-disclosing. The correct amount and content of self-disclosure is difficult to prescribe. It is important to remember, however, that consultants exist to enhance the experiences of consultees. Using this as a guiding principle suggests that consultants tell about themselves when personal information will inform or support the consultee.

Consultee: I know it's stupid. Half the people in the country are getting divorced, but I feel I've failed my own children and am terrified about what my school kids are going to think when they find out.

Consultant: You have to give yourself some time to get used to the idea of being divorced. Wait and see what's different and what's not in terms of your family and the class.

Consultee: I feel like I'll never be the same.

Consultant: I felt that way for the first few months after my divorce. In retrospect, I guess it's an unavoidable step in the grieving process. The feelings changed for me. I hope they'll change for you even sooner.

Consultants can build referent power (i.e., influence based on the perception that the consultee and consultant are enough alike that the consultant's suggestions are likely to be valid) with consultees by being self-disclosing so they are not mysterious or threatening to the consultee. Being open about past professional experiences, family members, hobbies, and so on is a way to connect with a consultee.

Consultants should avoid personal information that may be a burden to a consultee (e.g., family crises, history of illness, stress from work). They should not tell consultees things about themselves that may limit their influence with them. It's usually best to keep strong political or religious beliefs as private information. A history of substance abuse or mental disorder does not make a person unfit to be a consultant but can make a consultee uneasy about accepting advice.

Consultants who view themselves positively are probably most comfortable in self-disclosing. People with high self-esteem are easier to like, more influential with others, and more at ease with themselves.

High self-esteem supports resiliency or the ability to bounce back from stressful or traumatic incidents. Stress and disappointment are frequent companions to even the most knowledgeable and skillful consultants. An old family therapy adage suggests that it is not the number of problems that differentiate troubled versus happy families, but the coping mechanisms available to each family. Quick recovery from difficult situations is a vital quality for successful consultants as well.

Interactional Skills

Whether in a dyad or in a small group, the consultant should be expert at pursuing issues. This skill has at least two elements. First, the consultant can recognize important themes in a conversation and bring these back to people's awareness so they can be appropriately deliberated. Further, the skill includes an element of courage. Often, delicate, sensitive information is introduced into a group but then not discussed because members fear conflict. A willingness to pursue such an issue may be useful in helping a group or person confront difficult situations.

Consultants who deny they are ever angry or feel aggressive toward consultees or clients are probably deluding themselves. It's not whether we get angry, but how we get angry. Feedback and direct and indirect confrontation have already been discussed. It is critical that consultants use these techniques when they are upset rather than resort to indirect, sarcastic, or punitive forms of interaction.

Some unpleasant interactions must be accepted as part of working with people. Not every insult, slight, thoughtlessness, and so on deserves consultant attention. If such events are rare, they are likely dealt with best by ignoring them and going on. If they are frequent, further investigation is needed to determine whether the setting is appropriate for consultation and/or what part the consultant is playing in arousing such hostility. Table 2.1 lists potential pitfalls of consultation practice. In addition, consult Appendix A for some transcripts of consultation sessions. These may illustrate the techniques that have been described thus far.

ETHICAL CONSIDERATIONS IN
CONSULTATIVE PRACTICE

Professional and personal ethical codes guide consultant behavior. The translation of these codes into daily decisions can be difficult. Consultants do not have a particular set of rules that govern their basic behavior apart from the rules in effect for their other professional functions. The situations they find themselves in, however, are often complex because of the triadic nature of consultation, involving client, consultee, and consultant.

It is an impossible task to answer, in an a priori way, all ethical prob-

Table 2.1. Twelve Easy Steps for Failure as a Mental
Health Consultant

1. Know it all.
2. Learn nothing about the consultee.
3. Be unaware of your own motives.
4. Be definite, dogmatic, unyielding.
5. Sulk when your advice is not taken.
6. Use ambiguity to your own advantage.
7. Avoid feedback mechanisms.
8. Keep professional status in the forefront.
9. Conspire to cause unwanted, unsanctioned change.
10. Form alliances with subgroups.
11. Pick a few consultees as therapy patients.
12. Interpret consultees' motives with all available
   jargon.

Note. Adapted from Q. Rae-Grant, "The Art of Being a Failure as a
Consultant," in *Practical Aspects of Mental Health Consultation,* edited by
J. Zusman & D. L. Davidson (Springfield, IL: Charles C Thomas,
1972).

lems. Careful consideration of predictable dilemmas before they arise,
however, allows for some straightforward, self-confident action if and
when the situation calls for it (e.g., Lambert & Cole, 1977).

Who Is the Client?

A consultant has an obligation to work for the welfare of and protect
the information shared by consultees. The basic professional contract is
between these two. The needs of the client must also be acknowledged,
however. In addition, the consultant is often being paid by a system to
provide services. The individuals who hired the consultant can make legitimate accountability demands on the consultant.

Ethical issues arise when the rights of one member of this triad (client,
consultee, employer) seem to interfere with the rights of another. For
example, if the consultant observes a consultee do some form of harm to
a client, does the consultant owe primary allegiance to the consultee or the
client? If the employer seeks information about the job performance of a
consultee, should the consultant share perceptions if the consultee is, in
fact, incompetent?

Most consultants face some variant of the foregoing questions. What
are useful guidelines in making such decisions?

Confidentiality. Except in cases of illegal behaviors or situations that suggest
harm to self or others, consultants are bound to keep confidential what
they learn in a consultation relationship. As a general rule, prevailing moral
and legal standards must be abided by. A consultant cannot condone any
act that is inhumane or abridges the civil rights of another.

Following this general rule, then, whatever a consultant learns from a consultee is kept confidential unless the consultant is convinced that silence is apt to cause harm to the consultee, client, or some other individual. Obviously, identifying those situations that call for a breach in confidentiality is not always easy. In chapter 1 the diffuse line between consultation and supervision was mentioned. In situations that are apt to cause harm, a consultant may have to be directive and evaluative toward a consultee.

Assume that a consultant observes a consultee being remiss in the performance of a job (e.g., a teacher who is not prepared for class or a manager who is careless in monitoring work flow). The performance problem is not something to report to a supervisor (employer of consultant), but rather a potential target for consultation intervention.

On the other hand, a consultant who observes a teacher treat a child inhumanely or illegally (e.g., emotional abuse or, in some states, physical punishment) must report this behavior. Such reporting is made all the more critical if the consultee has refused to modify the illegal or inhumane behavior after a direct confrontation by the consultant.

Informed Consent. The basis of an ethical consultation relationship rests with the consent of each member of the relationship to agree to its parameters. The basic parameters are confidentiality, nonsupervisory interaction, and freedom to accept or reject advice or participation in the relationship. The best consultation probably occurs when confidentiality is promised. If confidentiality cannot be promised, however, consultation can proceed as long as all members understand this proviso. That is, if the consultant informs the consultee that in addition to the aforementioned constraints the consultant is required to report on the content of the consultation sessions to the organizational head, and the consultee agrees, no ethical violation has occurred when the consultant reports.

If the consultant informs the consultee that failure to experiment with consultation suggestions may be used as a basis for a future job evaluation, the consultee can determine whether the consultation relationship is worth the added burden of mandated use of advice. Many may decide against participating with such a regulation, but those who do participate do so understanding the demands.

Consultation cannot occur, however, if consultees are not free to choose participation. If consultees cannot reject participation in the relationship, they cannot give informed consent. Consultants must not work in settings where consultees are forced to interact with them. Such coercion is not always easy to detect. There can be subtle influences that make consultees feel they will suffer negative consequences if they reject a consultant's services or advice.

Some organizations which seek the services of an OD specialist, for example, exert pressure on employees to complete questionnaires or interviews. The OD consultant must be vigilant that information gained from data-gathering strategies is kept anonymous or that those giving the information know ahead of time that others will be privy to their answers.

Children are not usually in a position to reject the services of a consultant because the services are indirect. Because children by law and in practice do not give informed consent to consultation, their rights and needs deserve special attention. As potentially the most vulnerable member of the consultation relationship, their rights to confidentiality, privacy, nondiscriminatory assessment, best available treatment, and so on are all of the utmost importance to consultants. Some of the special considerations associated with consulting about children (in schools or other agencies) are discussed next.

Children and consent for treatment. Some organizations have been so concerned with the child's inability to give informed consent for consultation that they have assumed that parents must consent before teachers or other child caregivers can discuss a child with a consultant. This is a mistake.

Laws guaranteeing parent access to records and due-process safeguards protect the rights of children and their families. Their intent is not to prevent professional problem solving regarding the learning, behavioral, social, or emotional concerns of children. In schools, good teaching has always involved using educational resources, whether materials or people, to the fullest. Educators, mental health professionals, medical personnel, and so on have historically consulted with each other across grades and departments to clarify their thoughts about a child or to generate additional strategies for meeting each child's unique needs.

This problem-solving function is the role of the consultant. The consultant is bound by strict rules of confidentiality. The teacher-child concerns brought up in consultation are examined by the consultant and teacher searching for new alternatives, a different perspective, or the existing strengths of a child.

To increase their understanding of a problem, consultants may wish to observe in classrooms. No direct services are offered to the child without parental notification and permission. No decision about changing a child's educational program or placement is made by a teacher and a consultant. Decisions concerning new teaching or behavior management strategies may be made by teachers following consultation. These decisions and changes are typically within the province of teachers to make to enlarge their skills as educators. If consultation suggested that direct work with a child was necessary (e.g., evaluation, counseling, change in program), parent permission would be necessary to follow through on the appropriate course of action.

Typically, consultation interviews result in no reports or written records that must be added to the child's cumulative folder. The teacher and consultant may note important points in their discussion, promising strategies, or plan components, but no diagnostic classification concerning the child is ever recorded.

Discussion between the teacher and consultant should not be interpreted as a way to avoid getting parent permission about important elements in the educational process. Ideally, the school consultant would be introduced at a Parent's Night or Parent-Teacher Association (PTA) meeting and be available to explain the consultation role to parents. Schools that have consultation services might notify all the parents of the resource available to them and their children. Parents can be told that the consultant will be used to facilitate professional problem solving about their children's educational needs.

Children's and families' rights to confidentiality and informed consent are best protected by a professional staff committed to protecting these rights, careful of the quality of the information included in written records, and who discuss children in problem-solving, professional ways. Staff members must refrain from unkind or thoughtless evaluative comments that color the perceptions of others about a child or family. The intent of open records legislation is best served by a faculty that concentrates on the strengths of its children and shares information only with those who need to know to better educate a child.

Responsibility

The consultant is individually responsible for meeting moral, legal, and ethical standards. No agency policy or mandate is sufficient to reduce a consultant's personal obligation to provide competent services in an ethical manner to consultees and clients.

This standard suggests that consultants must be discriminating in choosing their work sites. Although consultants can work within an organization to improve its practices, they must not engage in any activity themselves that does not meet their highest professional standards.

Because behavior is the product of the interaction between an individual and a context, consultants should be wary of working for organizations whose values are not congruent with their own. Just as we would avoid toxic environments (e.g., poor air quality, dangerous substances), consultants might acknowledge that their ethical decision making could be impaired by working in unethical contexts.

Competence

The term *consultant* is generic. Consultants must be scrupulous in informing consultees about their special credentials and exact titles, if any.

The sources of consultant competence (e.g., educational history, professional experiences) should be made available to consultees. For example, if the title Educational Consultant is used, consultants should inform their consultees what degrees they have earned, where or how they gained knowledge about educational practices, and in what specific areas of education they can make expert contributions.

Consultants must never exceed the limits of their competence or mislead consultees regarding their expertise. Consultants can seek supervision to enlarge their repertoires or engage in additional study, but they must analyze every consultation request in light of what they really know. That no one person can have mastery of the entire domain of any field (e.g., psychology, special education, business management) is difficult for some practitioners to accept.

A corollary of a concern for competence is restraint in the quality of public statements consultants make about themselves. They cannot make false claims for effectiveness of their services or imply that they deliver higher quality services than other consultants unless they have actual data to support such claims. If consultants do disseminate evaluative information about their effectiveness, they must be careful to avoid bias in their presentation.

Welfare of Clients

Client and consultee needs must go before the needs of the consultant or the organization. Consultants must do no harm to their consultees and clients. Some of the implications of this statement were discussed in the foregoing section, "Responsibility." Others concern the inconvenience of being involved with humans and balance between legitimate and competing needs in a relationship.

One developmental tension that is constantly recapitulated over the life span is that of autonomy versus interdependence or dependence and independence (Kegan, 1982). This tension is a personal challenge for every consultant and every human and is inherent in every consultation relationship. How much does a consultant do for a consultee; how available is the consultant; what extra efforts are appropriate?

It is important to acknowledge that consulting is a demanding endeavor. Working with stressed people can be difficult. Flexibility, a willingness to adapt, and extra effort are all important characteristics of a good consultant. Going the extra mile, however, is not the same as allowing or encouraging a consultee to exploit a consultant. The consultant may need to know the difference between being helpful to others and encouraging dependency. Supervision can also help consultants to keep focused on what legitimate demands they can make on consultees.

Professional Relationships

Consultants must be willing to involve others in their work. Facilitating helpful resource networks for consultees is a vital consultation function. There should be no turf guarding among consultants, because their only function is to be useful to their consultees. An ideal consultant is respectful of the professional competence of colleagues, talented in building instrumental professional relationships, and characterized as always giving credit where due.

Dual Relationships

While maintaining rapport and trusting relationships with consultees, consultants must be sensitive to dangers associated with dual relationships. These include mixing psychotherapy with consultation and romantic relationships with consultees.

Although the lines between consultation and counseling are somewhat diffuse, wise consultants continuously try to avoid becoming entangled in intense therapy interactions with consultees. Keeping focused on work, explaining the differences between therapy and consultation, displacing discussions away from the consultee, and referring consultees to outside agencies are all ways of avoiding contaminating one role with another.

Consultants can attend group social events with consultees, but more personal relationships must be avoided. Even successful love affairs between a consultant and consultee put the consultant in a different organizational niche. The consultant becomes aligned with a certain person or group in the system and therefore can lose effectiveness with other groups or factions. Unsuccessful love affairs can be disastrous if scorned lovers decide to provide the rest of the system with all the gruesome details.

Interventions

All treatment has ethical issues surrounding it. Important questions are (a) Is it safe? (b) Is it appropriate? (c) Is it the best available? Interventions based on every theoretical approach have been analyzed using ethical standards. Treatment grounded in social learning theory may deserve special attention because it guides much of the work of school-based consultants.

First, some behavioral interventions rely mainly or solely on environmental modification instead of personal change. This may make people feel that they are mere products of their environment. Behavioral jargon also suggests that the client is more of a target of the procedure than a partner in the treatment.

Secondly, behavioral procedures are successfully applied when the interveners have control of environmental contingencies. This implies withholding and presenting positive and negative consequences (or adapting antecedent conditions) to increase the likelihood that a particular behavior will be accelerated or reduced. Control of another's reinforcements and punishments raises ethical issues if client control of outcomes is not clearly outlined. Skinner (1974) noted that people will not work or change for negative consequences and so there is little chance of aversive control becoming the preferred methodology. Children and other limited-informed-choice clients (e.g., prisoners, mentally retarded) are often not partners in choosing the treatment, however, and so it becomes unclear, even when positive contingencies are used, for whom the consultant is working.

Behavioral consultants are warned against dead-person targets. That is, they should not develop a management program that aims at promoting behaviors best done by dead people—sitting still, being quiet, being passive. Dead-person targets increase caretaker ease but do not enhance clients' coping abilities.

Well-conceived management programs must also examine what the minimal reinforcing and maximal aversive stimuli will be. It is both practical and ethically sound to do less rather than more as long as such interventions are equally effective. Children should not be led to believe that unnecessarily dramatic positive outcomes will follow relatively routine behaviors. Neither should they experience aversive consequences for minor infractions. If significant environmental changes are necessary to establish a new behavior while extinguishing others, the fading of the contingencies should be carefully planned. Fading should not imply, however, a return to a noncontingent environment.

A third issue revolves around the adaptiveness or usefulness of behaviors targeted for change. Behavioral consultants are quick to notice what secondary gains follow from the occurrence of a behavior that appears to be dysfunctional. Theoretical and applied work in family therapy have suggested that dysfunctional behavior in any system is related to that system's problems rather than residing singularly within the labeled person (e.g., de Shazer, 1985; Hoffman, 1981). Thus, it is important to conceptualize how deviant behavior is useful to certain systems.

Sometimes changing a child's behavior is inefficient because the system will constantly create new impaired members. Research on families (Minuchin, 1974; Minuchin, Rosman, & Baker, 1978) has shown that when one identified patient is removed from the family, frequently another child or one of the spouses begins to show symptoms (i.e., troubling behaviors). Symptoms, therefore, have reinforcing consequences for more than the individual with the symptoms. Effective (and therefore ethical) practice demands that the entire system surrounding a troubled client be examined before a behavior change program is implemented.

Although this section highlights a discussion of ethics and behavioral techniques, similar concerns should be raised about every treatment regimen. For example, the continued use of techniques that do not result in reductions of problematic behaviors or assessment strategies that do not suggest treatment options must be questioned on ethical grounds.

Dilemmas or Difficulties

An ethical dilemma is the result of two codes coming into conflict. For example, can the consultant break a child's confidence when a parent demands to know the content of their interactions? Kohlberg's (1964) formulations about levels or stages in moral thinking highlight the complexity involved in making personal choices. Kohlberg, like Piaget, conceptualized people as moving through increasingly abstract and inclusive stages of thinking about moral decisions. It is important, therefore, for consultants to reflect not only on legalities but also on what personal beliefs about rightness and wrongness are broadcast by the actions. Every action (and reaction) broadcasts a value.

There are, of course, difficult things to do (for example, confront a consultee) that are not to be confused with moral dilemmas. Just because it is difficult to do something does not make it an ethical question requiring days of pondering and much expert supervision. All dilemmas are difficult, but not all difficulties are moral dilemmas. Difficulties arise and must be confronted directly and quickly. For example, if the consultant learns that a consultee is unhappy with his or her services, the consultant must approach that consultee to try to reestablish rapport and credibility. The consultant must not obsess for days about the information.

In addition, just because something is difficult to do (e.g., offer services to an unappreciative consultee, get unfair feedback, or find resources for people who will not use them), consultants must not give up. Ethics add to tenacity (Newland, 1981). Consultants perform difficult tasks under trying circumstances because they know they are doing the right thing. The circumstances do not define what is fair and just. Each consultant defines the standards of goodness and justice, and these standards are how others will know the consultant.

SUMMARY

The skills necessary to begin a consultation relationship include communication, personal and group process skills, problem solving, and ethical decision making. Along with special content expertise, these skills combine to create a professional who knows information important to the resolution of the problem situation, can involve others in a problem-solving stance toward complex issues, engenders the confidence and trust of others so they stay involved in treatment efforts, and is flexible enough to work in many different formats with a wide array of consultees.

SUGGESTED READINGS

Anderson, T. K., Kratochwill, T. R., & Bergan, J. R. (1986). Training teachers in behavioral consultation and therapy: An analysis of verbal behaviors. *Journal of School Psychology, 24,* 229–241.

Bowers, N. E. (1971). Some guidelines for the school psychologist in his attempts to intimidate the teacher during a conference. *Journal of School Psychology, 9,* 357–361.

Burke, J. P., & Ellison, G. C. (1985). School psychologists' participation in organization development: Prerequisite considerations. *Professional Psychology: Research and Practice, 16,* 521–528.

Curtis, M. J., & Zins, J. E. (1988). Effects of training in consultation and instructor feedback on acquisition of consultation skills. *Journal of School Psychology, 26,* 185–190.

Gallessich, J. (1985). *The profession and practice of consultation.* San Francisco: Jossey-Bass.

Hughes, J. N. (1986). Ethical issues in school consultation. *School Psychology Review, 15,* 489–499.

Chapter 3

Targets and Operational Levels

Chapter 2 discussed skills and attitudes needed to initiate and maintain consultative services. This chapter also discusses consultation skills, but from the perspective of the particular operational level or target of the consultation program.

Operational level refers to the system in which the consultant is working to facilitate change. *Target* refers to the person, group, or issue the consultant is working to help. The operational level and target may be the same; for example, the consultant may be working with a consultee to increase the consultee's skills and knowledge. Level and target may differ, however, in cases where the consultant is working with a principal to create change in a school system's morale.

Although it is somewhat imprecise to identify specific skills as unique to particular working levels or targets, this way of organizing a discussion of skills may assist in further refining the reader's understanding of an ecological approach to consultation. What follows, then, are particular emphases that a consultant would adopt in working with microsystem, mesosystem, and macrosystem levels.

INDIVIDUAL OR MICROSYSTEM WORK

Individuals must be seen as complex systems of emotions, cognitions, conscious and unconscious motivations, behaviors, and reactions to environmental stimuli. The individual has a learning history, expectations about future events, a set of and propensity toward certain kinds of attributions, and is at a particular developmental point in his or her life span. In addition, the individual is embedded in a life space (Lewin, 1951) with forces that support or impede change efforts. The smallest unit of analysis and change in consultation is the life space jointly (and reciprocally) occupied by the consultee, client, and consultant.

As a matter of convenience, a consultant may begin searching for questions and solutions in this life space, the microsystem. Microsystem assessment, diagnosis, and intervention are critical consultation skills.

Assessment Processes

During an initial interview, consultants must formulate the consultation problem. Consultees often have conceptualized the problem in a way that defies resolution. Consultants must be aware of the consultees' formulations, client characteristics, and a host of other factors that enter into a sophisticated diagnostic process.

Table 3.1 lists questions that require attention before the consultation problem can be identified.

As illustrated by the questions listed in Table 3.1, the goal of the initial interview (and every interview) is for the consultant to be sensitive to the

Table 3.1. Microsystem Assessment in Consultation

Questions About the Consultee
  What factors are creating difficulty for the consultee?
    Lack of skills? Which ones?
    Lack of knowledge? What domains?
    Lack of professional objectivity? Why?
    Impaired feelings of self-efficacy? Why?
    Unsuccessful history of solving this problem?
    No readiness to engage in consultation?
    Unsuccessful history with this or another consultant?
    An organization that does not support consultation?
    A problem that is severe and/or bizarre?
Questions About the Client
  What factors are creating difficulty for the client?
    No environmental support to make a behavioral change?
    Irrational beliefs about a situation?
    Tasks that do not match current skills and knowledge?
    Temperamental qualities that do not match the environment?
    Learning history that inhibits acquisition of new behavior?
Questions About the Relationship Among Consultant, Consultee, and Client
  What factors could create difficulties for the consultant?
    What is the role the consultant assumes vis-à-vis the consultee?
    What are the consultant's needs in the consultation relationship?
    What is the consultant's history of success in dealing with this problem?
    What knowledge must be identified before the problem can be addressed?

array of issues that enter into the way problems are conceptualized, presented, and eventually solved. Consultants must always ask themselves the following questions:

1.   What are other ways of seeing this problem? Although my research may support my methods as most efficacious, are they likely to be adopted by this other professional?

2.   What will be seen as success from the perspective of the consultee and the client? Can I accept that, or do their perspectives underestimate (or overestimate) the change potential in this situation? Do I ask people to change more or less than they want to change? How do I do this?

3.   How does my history with problems like these color my problem formulation and resolution vision? Does this problem seem minor in relation to my experience or bizarre and intense? Does either perception change my approach or my expectations for success?

The consultant can use an array of assessment strategies to assist in the formulation of the consultation problem. Interviews, observations, standardized and nonstandardized tests, and analysis of archival data are all possibilities. A consultant can investigate teachers' lack of skills and knowledge through interviews and observations.

If a consultee is reluctant to engage in the consultation process, this may be because of a lack of readiness (i.e., Does this person have collaborative problem-solving skills or accept the premise that he or she should seek peer support for a problem?), an unsuccessful prior history with consultation, or an unpleasant association with the current or past consultants. If the consultee is simply not ready for consultation, the consultant must target giving those skills to the consultee before pursuing a case-centered strategy. If the consultee has rejected the idea that peer problem solving will be helpful, then the consultant must have a strategy to improve the consultee's expectations regarding the relationship between them.

Gerald Caplan's (1970) work is most complete in terms of elaborating on individual work with consultees. He advised the consultant to be sensitive to consultee cognitive and affective variables.

Interventions for Loss of Professional Objectivity

Caplan (1970) considered the loss of professional objectivity to be the most salient of consultee problems. When consultees are failing with a case despite having the requisite skills, knowledge, and self-esteem to be successful with similar cases, the consultant should consider Caplan's framework. He suggested that professional objectivity is impaired by direct personal involvement, simple identification, transference, attributional distortions, or theme interference.

Problem solving, clarification, modeling appropriate affect, and reality testing with the consultee are appropriate strategies to deal with all but the final two of these problems. Personality disorders might require referral outside the consultee's agency for therapeutic help or may be so minor that they do not affect the overall effectiveness of a consultee.

A theme is an unconscious conflict related to a consultee's life experiences or fantasies that has been unsatisfactorily resolved. The theme takes the form of a syllogism involving an inevitable link between two items or statements; there is an *Initial Category* followed by an *Inevitable Outcome*. Ellis and Harper (1975) described how people link an antecedent with a behavioral consequence without considering the irrational belief that actually creates the consequence, and Caplan suggested that consultees' irrational and unconscious beliefs interfere with their typical professional effectiveness.

Theme interference reduction is accomplished in three phases: assessment of the theme, consultant intervention, and follow-up and ending (Caplan, 1970). Identifying problems in objectivity, self-efficacy, or irrational attributions requires some sophistication. The clues include strange lapses in competence in handling client problems by consultees who are typically skilled; intense emotionality in describing cases; unusual fascination with the details of a case; relating personal or somewhat tangential information in the problem description; and discrepant nonverbal cues indicating anxiety during the case discussion.

Interventions for decreasing the themes include verbal focus on the client, verbal focus on an alternative object (the parable), nonverbal focus on the client, and nonverbal focus on the relationship.

Verbal Focus on the Client. Verbal focus on the client involves the consultant providing alternatives not present in the consultee's inevitable outcome. Without disputing the consultee's apparent problem formulation, the consultant adds other possibilities for endings.

> *Case Example.* The consultee was a member of a religious group that valued women in traditional homemaker roles and emphasized the superiority of male decision making. She was also an educational supervisor. She reported her panic at confronting, again, a male special education teacher. She was sure that he would defy her, solicit and receive his principal's support, and that she would become angry and behave inappropriately. Agreeing that all this was possible, the consultant suggested that if the male teacher were approached with concrete suggestions, he might also ask for clarification, try out some of her suggestions, and come to see her as a valuable resource. In

addition, the consultant said that the consultee might want to use her anger strategically in some situations to show her own convictions and at other times model calmness when under stress.

The themes involved here include the following: (a) Men in subordinate positions to women will always be rebellious and receive covert support from the powerful men in the environment; (b) female supervisors are hysterical and ineffective in the face of male defiance; and (c) women who seek supervisory positions are always unsuccessfully trying to emulate men, which is against the natural order of things.

Parable. Caplan's (1970) psychodynamic orientation caused him to warn against bringing the consultee's realization of the personalized interfering theme to consciousness. If the consultant feels that focusing on the case too specifically will cause the consultee's personal involvement to become apparent, the consultant can tell a story.

A well-designed story accomplishes the same goal as verbally focusing on the client; that is, it provides alternatives to the inevitable outcome. The story moves the consultee away from the present case and prevents the consultee from becoming the focus of this problem. The displacement of the problem from the consultee to the client is retained.

> *Case Example.* In the case just described involving the female supervisor, the consultant hesitated to delve into the supervisor's feelings and strategies too much because of the consultant's assumption of the presence of deeply ingrained religious conviction. The consultant, also a female, decided that a parable might be in order. She jokingly told the consultee of her own efforts to supervise young, bright, male and female doctoral students in psychology. The consultant recounted some of her own misadventures, how she had to learn supervisory skills—they had not been specifically taught—and finally how, although there had been one clear failure on the consultant's part, there had been 100 or so seemingly successful relationships. The consultee relaxed immediately, agreeing that trial-and-error learning was unavoidable but that most mistakes could be overcome.

A further note on parables may be appropriate. Some consultation practitioners have objected to storytelling when the story is in whole or part fabricated. The strategy has seemed dishonest or ungenuine to some. After a little experience, most consultants have a repertoire of true stories to tell that may serve the purpose. In addition, the parable is never told to mislead or provide incorrect information to a consultee. It is told as a way to communicate more effectively. Young consultants may wish to use the parable sparingly, as its face validity may be questionable given their obviously limited experience. On the other hand, some young consultants are expert in developing believable and useful stories that suit the situation at hand.

The late and renowned scholar of myths, Joseph Campbell (1968, 1974) might be read by consultants interested in the historical significance of the parable or the myth. His work, although far afield from school consultation, provides a framework for understanding what people wonder about and have difficulty incorporating into their lives. His use of myth to depersonalize attributions of goodness and badness might be particularly useful to consider. For example, he recounted myths and legends of ancient cultures all over the world that show the integral relationship between heros and villains and that these roles are often indistinguishable.

Nonverbal Focus on the Case or the Consultation Relationship. In addition to words, the consultant expresses an estimation of the case severity and an evaluation of the consultee in every action and reaction. A consultant's calm, respectful facial expression can have a significant effect on a consultee's handling of a case.

The skills discussed in chapter 2 regarding careful listening, egalitarianism, and maintenance of appropriate anxiety levels are critical for reducing consultee emotionality toward a case and toward a consultant. These skills also accomplish what Caplan (1970) called one-downsmanship. This is a process of keeping the relationship an egalitarian, peer-oriented interaction by downplaying the consultant's a priori knowledge and emphasizing consultees' expertise and resources to handle a problem.

Summary. One microsystem target in consultation is dealing with consultee attributions and affect. Theme interference may or may not be an outgrowth of the consultee's unconscious conflicts. Some consultants might prefer Ellis and Grieger's (1977) conceptualization of irrational beliefs rather than unconscious dynamics. Ellis's Rational Emotive Therapy (RET) involves the therapist in continued confrontation of the client's distorted beliefs or catastrophizing. Meyers et al. (1979), in describing their views on theme reduction, suggested more direct confrontation of the consultee than Caplan (1970) recommended.

Care must be taken, however, not to damage rapport with consultees. Consultants must work within the constraints of somewhat brief relationships. Some of the indirect methods suggested by Caplan, regardless of the source of the problems, are not threatening to the consultee-consultant interaction and may be preferable to direct confrontations. Time is an important factor to consider. Will there be time to rebuild a relationship that has been damaged by a consultee's defensiveness?

Clients' Microsystems

Another way to conceptualize microsystem assessment is to use Lewin's (1951) construct of life space to organize data collection. What are the forces in the immediate environments of the consultee and client that are

supportive of problem resolution and that would inhibit resolution? These
forces are people, history, technology, expectations, climate, and so on.

Case Example. Tyler is a junior-high-school student of average intelligence
who is failing some subjects and being mildly disruptive in several classes.
His parents are divorced, and he lives with his mother and stepfather.

Following extensive assessment, the consultant who has been asked to
assist in treatment planning for this youngster organized her information as
shown in Table 3.2.

An analysis of supportive or driving forces suggests areas of interventions involving enhancement, while an analysis of inhibiting forces suggests areas for remediation. The analysis also pinpoints the people in
Tyler's life whose behaviors or attitudes interact with his behavior and
attitudes. Some of Tyler's difficulties are predictable and obvious (e.g.,
teenage problems with authority, behavior problems associated with divorce and single parenting, resentment toward the stepfather's encroach-
ment into the family unit).

An analysis of the driving and inhibiting forces in Tyler's life space
suggests that interventions are possible in both of Tyler's primary settings,
home and school (coordination of work across these settings would involve
mesosystem intervention). Both settings contain some strengths to build
on as well as some deficits to overcome (in all the people in the settings,
not only Tyler). Because Tyler was unmotivated to accept personal respon-

Table 3.2. Data Organization for Consultation

Supportive Forces	Inhibiting Forces
	School
Normal intelligence	Written language disability
	Lack of problem-solving strategies
Math aptitude	Undeveloped academic motivation
Some school success	Current problems in school
Desire to excel	Fear of failure and evaluation
Committed teachers	Low teacher skills in enforcing contingencies
	Peers
Circle of friends	Low-achieving peer group
Interest in girls	Immature understanding of relationships
Interest in sports	Problems with authority
	Family
Concerned mother	Disengaged biological father
Concerned stepfather	Conflict with stepfather
Affection for sister	History of disappointment with relationships
Affection for father	Idealized memories of father
	Medical
Well built, muscular	Some residual central nervous system (CNS) involvement
	Tyler
Specific high esteem	Anxiety about behavior
	Sadness over family structure
Likes to be needed	Hypersensitivity to criticism

sibility for his problems, changing the behaviors and attitudes of others may be the first choice for intervention.

Interventions to Modify the Environment

Expert use of the behavioral model allows the consultant to assist in creating environments for clients and consultees that will support positive change. To do so requires an intimate, flexible knowledge of behavioral programming and learning principles with all of the interpersonal skills and sensitivities mentioned in previous sections.

Amelioration of client problems, increased consultee skills in handling problem behaviors in clients, and the linking of psychological research to educational applications are all important outcomes when working at the microsystem level. The two areas of skill development to be pursued by consultants are content knowledge of behavior techniques and principles, along with the verbal skills in structuring the consultant-consultee interaction.

Interview Format. Bergan and his associates (1977; Bergan & Kratochwill, 1990; Tombari & Bergan, 1978) reported a fascinating research program in behavioral consultation. They proposed a four-step (or four-interview) framework. Behavioral consultants can structure interviews in phases: problem identification, problem analysis, intervention, and evaluation and follow-up.

Problem identification involves a mutual understanding between consultant and consultee of exactly what the problem is in behavioral, observable terms. The process of gaining this mutual understanding is more difficult than most consultants believe. It is the most critical element in the four-phase framework.

Once the problem is behaviorally described, the consultant and the consultee decide on a way to collect baseline data. This may involve the consultant in a few classroom visits, or it may be left entirely to the consultee. In either case, the procedure to collect the data must be carefully explained to the consultee. The consultant should not sit in a classroom taking notes without explaining to the teacher the purpose and the nature of the notes. Even self-confident teachers can experience some concern with an unexplained data collection method. At the least, consultants can provide teachers with copies of their checklists or some form of immediate feedback before leaving the classroom. If the teacher is establishing the baseline, the consultant should suggest the least time-consuming, easiest-to-understand data collection method. Additionally, the consultant should phone or drop by to support the teacher's efforts and provide suggestions to resolve unforeseen difficulties.

In the problem validation interview, baseline information is used to establish the existence of a problem and to begin designing an intervention strategy. Occasionally, a consultee's focused attention on a target behavior will result in the behavior no longer being seen as problematic. Either the frequency of the behavior is actually low, or its precipitant becomes obvious so the consultee can make the necessary adjustments in the classroom without further consultation.

The baseline data should also shed light on the antecedents and consequents of the target behavior. What precedes the behavior in terms of social context, teacher behavior, time of day, and subject matter? In addition, the consultant and consultee must analyze what follows the behavior so the contingencies maintaining the undesirable behavior may be modified.

The consultant and consultee may observe, for instance, that the child emits the target behavior most frequently when sitting alone, assigned to written work. They may also notice that one child's disruption is frequently followed by disruption from another small group, leading to teacher reprimands and a lengthy interruption of regular classroom activities. A child might find any part of that sequence reinforcing. The intervention plan designed by the consultant and consultee can make use of this information by altering antecedent and/or consequent conditions in hope of altering the unacceptable behavior.

The problem analysis phase must also include careful consideration of the resources available to bring to bear on the problem. These resources include the general organization of the classroom (small groups, learning centers, peer tutoring, movement, individualization, scheduling) and teacher skills or propensities (positive attention, games, artwork, attention to detail). In addition, resources outside the classroom might be identified such as parent involvement, other teaching or school staff support, a pre-referral team (see chapter 5 for a discussion of these teams), or reinforcements associated with visits to other classrooms or people and places in the community (most of these would be mesosystem interventions).

The problem analysis ends with a designation of an intervention in addition to a continued data collection process. The consultee and consultant delineate the discrepancy between actual and desired behaviors (in terms of kinds of behaviors or frequency or duration of behavior) and establish some tentative goals for the intervention to be deemed successful. These goals or desired behaviors deserve careful consultant attention.

It is important to compare a consultee's expectations of client's behaviors to developmental realities. First graders do not sit quietly for hours and hours working alone on written assignments. A program designed to accomplish such an anomaly invites frustration for everyone involved. Further, a child who has never been observed to emit a desired behavior (e.g., playing cooperatively with peers) is unlikely to display the behavior with any frequency.

Not only should consultees receive information about shaping and chaining behaviors, but they should also be encouraged to assume that change will take considerable time and effort. It is tempting to wish for instant success with carefully planned interventions. It is all right to wish, but not all right to give up on a strategy after only a few days. Most troublesome behaviors have been nurtured by unfortunate contingencies for years. It is unreasonable to assume that change will be rapid for a behavior that has already defied attempts to extinguish it.

During implementation of the mutually developed plan, the consultant should make contact with the consultee to offer support, suggestions for revision, and continued problem solving. Data collection must, of course, continue during the intervention phase.

Finally, after a specified time has elapsed, the consultant and consultee should meet to evaluate the effectiveness of their efforts. This meeting may result in a decision to extend the strategy, modify the plan, or completely recycle through the problem-solving process. Even though human service personnel believe that all problems, if understood, are amenable to change, this does not imply that the first change strategy will be effective. An openness to new ideas and even different problem conceptualizations is needed if consultants hope to increase problem-solving skills in themselves and others. Persistence and flexibility are crucial.

Verbal Structuring. Another aspect of implementing microsystem consultation is careful attention to the consultant's verbal statements. Such attention to consultant verbalizations is always important and has been most carefully researched in behavioral consultation (Bergan & Tombari, 1975, 1976; Tombari & Bergan, 1978). Caplan (1970) also reported on the effectiveness of the related concepts of unlinking (a process of splitting the initial category of a theme from its inevitable outcome) and theme interference reduction. Others analyzed verbal processes as stages of problem solving (e.g., Cossairt, Hall, & Hopkins, 1973; Friedman, 1978; Isaacson, 1981; Robbins, Spencer, & Frank, 1970; Wilcox, 1977); as indications of dominance in the consultation relationship (Erchul & Chewning, 1990); and as indicators of consultant expertness (Salmon & Lehrer, 1989). Each of these directions is promising, but as yet clear practice implications have not been established.

The Tombari and Bergan (1978) research illustrates how consultants' verbalizations affect consultee beliefs about a case. When given behavioral cues about a case, consultees reported more favorable impressions of prognoses than when given medical model cues. Such work points to the importance of the verbal influence process occurring during consultation. Other work by Bergan and Tombari (1975) suggests the importance of focusing on each of the consultee's topics thoroughly before moving on to new topics. Although more research is needed in this area, it seems accurate that consultants who can influence the content and direction of an interview in such a way as to stay on topic will be more successful than those who cannot do so.

The *Consultation Analysis Record* developed by Bergan and Tombari (1975) emphasizes several areas deserving verbal attention from the consultant. The consultant can elicit information from the consultee regarding the background environment of the client, the overt and covert behaviors of the client, and the present setting of the troublesome behavior. The consultant can also investigate the individual characteristics of the child, the personality traits, intellectual abilities, and physical descriptors. Behavioral consultants may tend to downplay verbalizations of individual characteristics in favor of eliciting the consultee's observations concerning overt behaviors. The consultant will also share statements concerning observational techniques with the consultee.

One finding of the Bergan and Tombari research program was that successful problem identification was highly related to plan implementation. In cases where plans were actually implemented, 95% were reported as successful. Thus, it is clear that effort expended on increasing the influence of consultant verbalization may be important for problem resolution.

SMALL-GROUP AND ORGANIZATIONAL CHANGE

Process Phenomena

Process refers to the way a certain event happens rather than what occurs. We may all arrive at grandmother's house for pudding, but some of us ride horseback over hills, others drive through snow, and some sail down rivers. The how and the what of human interaction are both crucial. It is important to learn the delicate balance between the two phenomena and to adjust the balance depending on the people involved, the task at hand, and the prevailing environmental stress.

The first obvious problem for the consultant working at a small-group level is becoming free from merely the content of what is occurring to enable observation and interpretation of process events. Table 3.3 lists some common processes that could be evident during any small-group activity.

Roles that people assume in groups facilitate or impede the task accomplishment and morale of a group. Task roles help get jobs done. Maintenance roles attend to the social and emotional well-being of a group. Individual roles interfere with group life as a member pursues a personal agenda (e.g., for power, revenge, attention, etc.) at the expense of the group.

Consultants rarely have difficulty recognizing group processes once

Table 3.3. Group Process Phenomena

Task	Maintenance	Individual
Emerging leadership	Gate keeping	Blocking action
Disagreeing	Encouraging	Defending
Time keeping	Harmonizing	Arguing
Agenda setting	Listening skills	Diverting
Consensus testing	Elaborating	Observing
Decision making	Offering help	Withdrawing
Initiating	Feedback skills	Blaming
Diagnosing	Clarifying	
Summarizing	Agreeing	
Calling for attention or action	Compromising	
Information or opinion seeking	Following	
Information or opinion giving	Tension releasing	
Standard setting and testing	Expediting	

they have been alerted to the existence of this dimension of interaction. Consultants must, of course, make some hypotheses concerning the relative usefulness of certain processes for a group and the costs or benefits derived from some processes being emphasized or ignored.

For example, the process consultant who observes no gate-keeping functions during staff meetings will, therefore, look to see what is going wrong for that group and decide if the lack of gate keeping may be part of the problem. Consultant attention to gate keeping is influenced by a belief that shared interaction during a meeting is a good thing.

Another dimension for the consultant to consider when interpreting group processes is the developmental stage of the group or individual group members (Schein, 1969). People seem to have qualitatively different needs surrounding group membership over time. The needs, in developmental order, concern clarity about membership, influence, feelings, individual differences, and productivity.

Membership. The first struggle a new member faces when entering a group is learning what it means to be a member. What are the norms, the advantages, and the costs? During this period, the consultant might observe a participant to be involved in relatively few initiating processes and far more information- and opinion-seeking activities. The pattern should not be overinterpreted by the consultant as indicating low initiating skills on the part of the new member. The particular pattern may be appropriate given the person's developmental moment.

Influence. After understanding group acceptance issues, many members turn their attention to influence issues. Who are the power "haves" and "have nots"? Is power seen as more important than the good of the group? During this phase, members may attempt influence strategies that parallel the existing patterns or question the decision-making structures that are currently in place. Effective group leaders accept this as a predictable event and try not to respond defensively to questions and suggestions for change. New members are likely to make mistakes about going through channels and getting required approvals. These behaviors would probably not be signals to the consultant of authority problems in the staff unless they were part of long-tenured members' repertoires.

Feelings. The affective response of the group to individual members is another issue that commonly surfaces during group life. Will the group be supportive and constructively critical? Are feelings considered appropriate topics for discussion? Do honest appraisals of agenda items occur only after meetings are over? Members who suddenly confront a group with many unresolved issues may be reflecting a newly discovered understanding that feelings will be taken seriously. A group may appear helplessly bogged down in maintenance functions at a certain point in history. Consultants must use their understanding of the group's time frame to decide whether to push for more task functioning or simply facilitate the affective events as they happen.

Diversity. In some ways, the three previous stages have emphasized becoming an integral, influential member of the group by learning its norms and responding to its structures. A more difficult stage, accomplished by few individuals or groups, is coming to appreciate members' differences. It is common for groups to be divided in smaller units that coalesce because of shared attitudes, experiences, and values. Group leaders may require coaching and support to attempt to maximize a group's differences. Different talents, levels of involvement, and ideologies could be openly accepted as part of the group's strength. They should not automatically elicit pressure to conform.

Productivity. The final issue members and groups face is that of productivity. All groups have some purpose. The way in which that purpose is lived or accomplished depends primarily on how the previous stages have been resolved. If members feel that membership in a particular group is not self-enhancing and that their attempts at influence and displays of feeling are rebuffed, it is unlikely that productivity will be high.

Summary of Group Development

Some writers have summarized the aforementioned stages by referring to groups' forming, storming, norming, and performing stages of development. This simple list reminds those consultants who work with small groups that team difficulties are to be expected and are not indicators that group work should be abandoned.

Role of Values

Some groups spend inordinate amounts of time arguing about what is better or who is right. This indicates that group production is likely to reflect the least common denominator rather than creative synergy. Lack of organizational values associated with diagnosing situations, working issues through, and receiving reactions for new ideas should be apparent to the consultant. Inordinate competition in an organization makes it unlikely that these standards will be met. Although consultants who work with small groups focus on the problems recognized by the organization, there is an additional focus because of the values associated with attention to process. Some of these values include attention to human concerns at the work place, a focus on the way work is done, emphasis on long-range rather than short-range planning as well as effectiveness, and an acceptance of perpetual diagnosis as an alternative to reliance on generalizations or principles as modes of operation (e.g., "We've always done it that way"). The values espoused by small-group consultants are often products of research on improving the quality and quantity of work (e.g., Baker & Wilemon, 1977; Burns, 1977).

Observation

Observation of small-group processes is best done when the consultant is not heavily involved in the meeting under scrutiny. It is not impossible to be participant and observer, but it is difficult, especially for new consultants. Even consultants who exclusively observe must be aware that their presence is a part of the group process of which they are mainly unaware. The questions consultants ask themselves when doing their process observations are as follows:

- Who is talking with whom?
- Are the verbal and nonverbal messages congruent?
- Who is systematically ignored or attacked?
- How does the group make decisions?
- Are there group data that are ignored (e.g., the angry tone used by some members while verbally acquiescing)?
- Do the participants seem to know what to expect?
- Is the time allotted to each agenda item sufficient to allow discussion and reasonable given the total meeting time, number of agenda items, and importance of particular agenda items?
- How effective is the leader in keeping the group on task and setting standards for accomplishment?

Small-group or process consultants and their consultees work collaboratively. The consultant relies on the consultee for the details of the organizational structure, climate, and norms and is constantly involved in a process of mutual problem formulation and solution generation. Of course, there is more to process consultation than observing a staff meeting and then presenting the participants with a detailed list of process observations and interpretations.

> *Case Example.* During a 3-day workshop on process consultation, the group of three presenters added an unplanned activity. One presenter went unannounced and unexplained from one small workshop group to another, jotting down observations about each group's task and maintenance processes. When the activity was over, the one presenter smugly detailed his sophisticated observations. He was greeted with silence, and the participants later reported feelings of defensiveness and unexpected vulnerability to observation.

Such reactions are typical, even when process consultants have been invited to make their observations known. It is tempting to establish an expert position by showing off special sensitivities, but in the long run this is counterproductive. It is better, if asked to share observations, to ask questions of the group about how they experience a certain process (e.g., decision making). A consultant might share a single observation and ask the group to decide if the process described is functional or dysfunctional to group goals. In the end, the consultant wants the group to be able to diagnose and change its own process. It is best to start the self-analysis and self-renewal activities as soon as possible. Nothing is gained by positioning the consultant as the expert observer and interpreter.

Consultants often suggest and facilitate process observation periods at the end of regular work meetings. In addition, the consultant might provide mini-didactic inputs on agency setting, gate keeping, or decision making. Some administrative coaching of the leader is often called for if she or he is deficient in certain leadership skills. Skills important for leadership are the ability to give credit to others generously, to be task-oriented, to display concern toward the staff's personal issues, to introduce ideas, to be eager for feedback, and to model risk taking. In addition, the leader should be able to move flexibly among the various tasks and maintenance processes listed in Table 3.3.

Staff meetings take up a substantial portion of time, so energy is well spent to make them as efficient, effective, and enjoyable as possible. Attention to the physical setting, amenities, agenda, chairperson responsibilities, and timing are all critical leadership functions.

Decision Making

It is important for the consultant to investigate decision-making styles. The group will have a preferred style; for example, voting, consensus, or minority rule (Schein, 1969). The leader will also have a particular style; for example, selling, telling, or consulting (Tannenbaum & Schmidt, 1958). Each style or pattern has costs and benefits that are more or less useful given the participants and the task.

When the group members expect that they will be involved in a decision or the task is complex enough to benefit from collaborative problem solving, the leader is well advised to govern in a relatively group-centered fashion. This involves delegating certain tasks, consulting, and joining with group members about problem formulation as well as problem solutions, and continually allowing the group to have decision-making functions. In certain groups, however, there is no expectation for participatory leadership. Therefore, group morale and leader evaluations will suffer if the leader does not adopt a more leader-centered decision working style. The leader might test ideas before a group but generally arrives with a problem formulation and asks for input concerning a circumscribed set of possible solutions.

When tasks are simple, leaders in participatory or authoritative cultures are expected to make decisions alone. They are also expected to act independently if the group is faced with a serious emergency. Procedures to be used in an emergency might be a product of group action, but no one expects a vote to be taken on whether to leave a burning building.

Consultants can use their observation time to discern if decision-making styles are interfering with high-level group functioning. One common problem is the "plop" decision. This concerns never really making a decision—just allowing the last comment to be seen as a group mandate. If consultants can direct participants to an analysis of their styles and preferences, positive change may occur.

Data Gathering and Simulation

It is convenient to separate a data-gathering stage from an intervention stage. The process of collecting information is in itself a form of intervention. Process consultants must be sure their research methodologies are consonant with their values and reflective of procedures the consultant would like to establish as aids to ongoing organizational self-analysis. Straightforward procedures that are protective of people's privacy and other group norms are best.

Typical data-gathering methodologies are observations, questionnaires, surveys, interviews, and simulations. As with all consultation modes, the process consultant must be as certain as possible that all the consultees are willing participants and informed as to the purpose of the activities. They must also be made aware of the limits of confidentiality. These conditions cannot be taken for granted. It is embarrassing to arrive at an organizational subsystem and realize the members are uninformed as to what the consultation effort is all about. Ignorance often facilitates resistance and paranoia. Neither of these, obviously, is helpful to the consultative goals.

Instruments. There are many published sources for organizational data-gathering instruments (e.g., Blake & Mouton, 1976, 1978; Halpin & Croft, 1963; Lippitt & Lippitt, 1975; Schmuck & Runkel, 1985). If questionnaires or surveys are a preferred methodology, these sources are efficient guides.

The data-gathering process can be conceptualized as another entry problem. Consultees must be identified and prepared to complete the instruments. They must be informed as to how they are likely to benefit from candid participation in what might be a time-consuming process. No instrument is fake-proof, and the consultant must devote time to planning ways of motivating people to cooperate with survey procedures. The best way, of course, is having the particular methodology chosen in a collaborative effort between the gatherers and the providers of information.

Interviews. The previous discussion is equally applicable to interview techniques. In small organizations, it is helpful for the consultant to talk with each member. In this way, the consultant can try to see the system from a number of perspectives and discover the incongruities between stated goals and actual organizational behaviors. The consultant should be willing to answer questions from consultees to model openness and begin the process of mutual problem solving. If interviewees appear reluctant to answer questions, the consultant must be prepared to provide a rationale for the anxiety-provoking questions and look for alternative ways for investigating troublesome organizational issues.

Most interviews are best done in a semistructured manner. All the consultees must be asked the same questions, but this may be done with a relaxed and friendly approach. The consultant can follow the consultees' lead to new content areas, especially if this suggests formerly undiscussed problems. Great care must be taken to ensure confidentiality across consultees.

Simulations. Asking a group to take on a complex role and complete a team or intergroup task is a powerful data collection technique. Simulations should be designed with organizational goals as the guideposts. Simulations may last minutes or days and involve just a few organizational members or entire organizations.

The debriefing period following the simulation is probably the most critical in terms of consultee learning. Nothing is gained if consultees do something (e.g., decide what to carry to the moon or create a new organization) and then do not get a chance to discuss their experiences. The consultant must allow sufficient debriefing time to facilitate positive learning.

Case Example. One group abruptly aborted a simulation that involved the creation of two organizations that negotiated for the use of resources and one team of process consultants. One of the process consultants became upset after receiving negative feedback from his organizations. Members of each simulated organization became increasingly suspicious of possible manipulations taking place. A remaining process consultant insisted the simulation be stopped because people were getting hurt. She wanted to get out of the roles that seemed to her to be distorting the group process.

A long debriefing session revealed the strong themes of conflict avoidance and low trust that had plagued this group for almost 6 months. These issues interfered with their performance of the creative tasks of which they thought themselves capable. Although group members were upset by the emotion of one of its members, they did not trust the group to be a source of support and nurturance.

If debriefing is not complete after group experiences such as the one just described, participants are likely to leave confused and upset rather than enlightened. Not all confusion and upset can be discussed away, but process consultants must make strong efforts at dealing with each person before allowing the group to break or move to another task.

Many process consultants and other OD specialists have made use of sensitivity training or encounter groups as part of their consultation programs. These experiences are not simulations but activities that aim to focus participant energy and attention. The usual strategy is for members to deal with each other only about issues currently existing in the group. The goals are often to facilitate members' learning about their impact on others and learning new ways to express their impressions of others. Well-run groups are often intense experiences and are literal laboratories of interpersonal phenomena. Learning about personal styles stemming from group experiences can be significant.

Consultants who are operating at a group level should be wary of overusing an encounter group strategy. Early in the history of encounter groups, it became apparent that personal change made by group participants faded as they returned to a nonsupportive environment. Family groups (i.e., entire staffs, or naturally occurring work groups that attend encounter groups) tend to be more successful in generalizing the new skills back to the original situation. It is questionable, however, whether interpersonal issues among colleagues should demand so much attention and whether trust and openness (the hallmarks of encounter) are the only or best predictors of organizational behavior.

People are also motivated by greed and competition. Training groups are necessary that focus on maintaining competition at tolerable levels rather than intervening as if honest encounter will solve all organizational ailments. Consultants must stay aware of their own biases when planning strategies. The consultee organization should not be fit into a particular package just because the consultant likes running encounter groups.

Intervention in Classroom Process

A recent assessment strategy and tool from Ysseldyke and Christenson (1987) illustrates a role open to the process consultant interested in classroom processes.

The Instructional Environment Scale structures an observer's analysis of the instructional processes established for a particular target child. For example, the observer makes note of a teacher's effectiveness in adapting instruction, creating a positive class climate, managing disruptions, providing feedback, facilitating academic engaged time, keeping a cognitive emphasis, providing relevant practice, checking on student understanding, using motivational strategies, projecting high expectations, and accomplishing instructional planning. The observer can then characterize the instructional environment created for target children and provide the teacher with specific feedback on his or her strengths and on areas in need of further refinement.

School-based consultants might find important applications of this scale when assisting general education teachers who mainstream children. Consultants could describe the advantages of such a feedback and renewal process and offer their services to teachers. The use of the observation system should be, of course, voluntary and not involved in the ongoing evaluation of teacher competency. Evaluations related to tenure, merit pay, and so on should be done by building administrators, not by consultants (Idol-Maestas, 1983).

MACROSYSTEM ASSESSMENT AND INTERVENTION

The role descriptors of child-oriented professionals always contain a call to advocate for change in societal laws, regulations, and norms (Berlin, 1975; Biklen, 1976; Conoley, 1981a; Conoley, 1981b; Gallessich, 1974; Hyman, 1975; Mearig, 1974, 1978; Stein, 1972). Most educational consultants, however, do not receive training in intervention beyond the small-group level. Many skills are needed ranging from typical therapy-like skills to law, public relations, and negotiating skills. Some of the skills or content areas usually ignored in typical graduate sequences but required for macrosystem change are law, organizing people, organizing events, media use, negotiation, and parent partnership. Other important skills are persuasive writing or speaking, building support networks, and tremendous tolerance for both ambiguity and conflict.

Law

Professional ethics are regulations governing a particular group. They mainly inform the members what not to do (e.g., American Psychological Association, 1979). Graduates of professional programs are often aware of only these regulations and those affecting licensure, confidentiality, and perhaps involuntary commitment and some child welfare laws. School psychologists are often well informed regarding the laws affecting the rights of children to public education and due-process procedures. Overall, however, it is rare to find a helping professional with a comprehensive knowledge of both the content and process of the law (Phillips, 1990). Such knowledge is indispensable, however. This is no small task and requires substantial study and involvement. Taylor and Biklen's (1979) work is a helpful source.

In addition, all state and federal branches will send information on request regarding each of their functions and on new regulations written to implement new laws. Litigation must also be monitored, as it can have a dramatic effect on the implementation of law. An example is the 1981 Supreme Court decision overturning a lower court's decision in 1977 to provide treatment and education to mentally retarded people in the least restrictive environment. This well-known lower court's decision had forced the Penhurst State School to begin a process of deinstitutionalization. Deinstitutionalization received support and funding through the 1975 Developmental Disabilities Act. Thus, the process of deinstitutionalization, so prized by families and advocates of that time, seemed protected by law and then was overturned in the Supreme Court decision (6–3).

Lawyers with specialties in certain fields are indispensable when planning macrosystem change. Workshops on legal issues are available but must also be screened. Many workshops focus more on the laws affecting the particular profession than with laws affecting clients.

One important aspect of the law is the guarantee for due process extended to citizens. Consultants are well advised to understand the exact implications of due-process procedures for a particular area of concern. When a child is suspected of having a disabling condition necessitating a change in educational programming, certain steps must be taken to ensure that due process has occurred. If parties involved in the process of changing a child's placement have failed to document or take the actions outlined in the due-process steps, there is cause to contest any decision reached by placement committees.

Organizing People

Of almost equal importance as legal knowledge for macrosystem consultation is skill in getting people together to work on projects. The power to change systems resides in an ability to get the right people or the right number of people involved in the change effort. People must be organized to create pressure or lobbying groups to tip the political balance.

Sometimes large groups are needed for demonstrations, write-ins, sit-ins, work slowdowns, referendums, packing public meetings, and so on. Sometimes strategic alliances must be engineered between groups that, although not large, are influential. If a parents' group can gain the support of even a few school board members, it is likely that the group's goals will be met.

In addition, there are basic managerial skills involved in macrosystem change. Publications, meetings, and public relations events must be coordinated. Staff and volunteers must be supervised and oriented. Agendas and priorities must be monitored closely to make sure key issues are addressed. Complex plans do not implement themselves; they require careful coordination and constant monitoring. When social issues are addressed, people on both sides of the issues are often angry and behave as if the force of their emotion and the rightness of their cause will overcome all obstacles. Being right, with all its relative meanings, is helpful but does not guarantee success. Both groups in a struggle usually feel that they are right. This leads to a stereotyping and derogation of the opposing group. Consultants are wise to avoid that trap and attempt to see the other group in all its complexity. Alinsky's (1946) warning, "In order to be part of all, you must be part of none" (p. 204), should be kept in mind. Such awareness will increase the power of the consultant's suggestions for interventions and increase the chances of the groups moving together in an alliance.

Cormick and Love (1976) described some role possibilities open to those interested in facilitating social change: activist, advocate, and mediator. The activist is directly involved in the movement. Advocates are facilitators of change or maintainers of status quo but are not actually members of the groups involved (e.g., parents of handicapped, presidents of oil companies). Mediators are acceptable in some limited way to all the disputing factors. These people work for mutual improvement to terminate the conflict.

All of these roles are available to any citizen. Consultants who involve themselves in social change efforts might move among the roles as the situation warrants.

Organizing Events

Much of the work involved in organizing events is accomplished through organizing people. Consultants must be aware of the kinds of events or actions that are possibilities (Biklen, 1974). An action is a "planned activity that will lead to social change" (p. 90).

Actions will be successful if they (a) reflect short-term and long-term goals, (b) are timely, (c) use the skills of the people committed to the change, (d) are well planned, (e) meet people's expectations, (f) educate others, (g) are consistent with public values, and (h) lead others to actions.

Within these parameters, only group creativity and research will limit the diverse array of possible actions. Public forums or meetings, marches, coordinated letter writing, media coverage or production, symbolic acts (e.g., draft card burnings or arm bands), boycotts, community education efforts, or model programs are all possibilities.

Using Media

Mass media probably represents the single most potent influence on today's world. Access to and skillful use of media channels to create a change in public opinion are vital for consultants.

Possible media projects include press conferences, public service announcements, educational videotapes, newspaper stories, appearances on local talk shows, free or easily accessed information publications, brochures, posters, or thematic children's art. Each of these media projects employs skills in organizing and identifying people and arranging the event or context to increase the effect, and each depends on careful research and groundbreaking. Newspaper reporters, for example, have some independence in submitting stories for publication. Identifying a reporter interested in or sympathetic to a particular cause and providing that person with information about events may result in free publicity. Radio and television stations must broadcast, free of charge, a certain number of public service announcements. Although these announcements are usually aired at odd hours, someone is always listening or watching. It is possible that the announcement could appear at a high-usage hour if it is well produced.

A less dramatic use of media is effective letter writing. The letters may be part of a write-in campaign or simply written by individuals seeking change or clarification from an agency. Some members of constituency groups may rarely write anything. Parents, for example, may need help in both the process and content of letter writing. Some useful guidelines (adapted from *Making School Work,* Massachusetts Advocacy Center and Massachusetts Law Reform Institute, 1975) are as follows:

1.   Most routine matters between a child and teacher do not warrant letter writing. Telephone calls and notes can be used to keep communication lines open.

2.   Letters should be sent and a copy kept when issues important to a child's educational development arise. Examples include (a) a serious disci-

plinary action or an accusation that a child has broken an important rule; (b) a request for an educational service not presently available to a child; (c) a request to inspect or receive information from a child's records; (d) when a parent believes a child is being mistreated; or (e) a request for a meeting or a hearing with agency officials about some issue.

3.   Letters should be sent to the person directly involved with the issue. If a satisfactory solution is not accomplished, additional letters may be sent with carbon copies sent to the supervisors of the people directly involved.

4.   Copies are essential. Photocopied letters are important in verifying what was said to whom on what date.

5.   It is often good practice to pay the extra amount demanded to send a letter by certified mail. This establishes proof that the letter was sent and received.

6.   Follow-up letters are often needed (a) after telephone conversations that have occurred because of an initial letter; (b) when an initial letter fails to elicit an adequate response; (c) when no response is made to an initial letter; and (d) after meetings with an agency official, to document what transpired at the meetings and record decisions made verbally.

Consultants should encourage people to write letters concerning problems that affect them personally. The consultant can suggest the form and procedure for letter writing.

Negotiation

Negotiation is used when any two groups with conflicting interests meet to discuss the issues that divide them (Taylor, 1979). Negotiation is not an easy or comfortable process. It demands a tolerance for both internal and external conflict. Members of a negotiating team must be in control of their tendencies to become angry, withdrawn, or feel guilty when confronted with opposing viewpoints. In addition, they must be able to continue on a planned course no matter how angry, unreasonable, or accusing the opposite side may become.

Taylor (1979) described critical elements in negotiation. Negotiation should occur after informal appeals have failed but before going public with demands. Premature publicity sometimes locks a group into a public position from which they are later unwilling to retreat. After a public stand, a group may feel that its image will be tarnished by a compromise or change in policy. A well-timed private meeting might have allowed a change to occur and the powerful group to save face.

Whenever possible, the negotiating team should represent a coalition of groups advocating for change. The school system from which change is sought is more likely to accede if it recognizes a broad-based concern about its policies. The more groups that show concern about an issue, the harder it is for a school to ignore these concerns.

The setting for the meeting should be specified by the concerned group of advocates. This group explains the purpose of the meeting and specifies which school officials should attend. The numbers of representatives at the negotiation session should be equal for both sides. The advocate group should reschedule the session if many unexpected school personnel arrive at the meeting.

To negotiate successfully, the advocates must be well prepared. Knowledge of the budget, priorities, policies, procedures, and goals of the school is necessary. Discrepancies between stated mission and actual behaviors can be specified.

Emotional control must accompany careful preparation of facts. Anger may be useful if strategically applied but generally will lower problem-solving skills. Advocates should not feel guilty about making demands, become defensive, or beg for concessions.

If possible, consultants should electronically record or transcribe the meeting events. Firm timetables and standards of action should be established. Following the meeting, the advocate group can send the school a letter describing what transpired and request a reply if there are discrepancies between the advocate's and the school's memories of the decisions or agreements.

Negotiators must be willing to confront vague promises or generalizations. It is often more comfortable to let items go undiscussed than to deal with delicate or controversial issues. Allowing generalizations to take the place of specific action plans is a serious mistake.

Finally, all members of a negotiating team must keep a long-range perspective on a problem. This implies being able to see small gains as steps toward desired goals. A coherent plan of action is necessary that uses negotiation as one strategy in overall efforts. In this way, small concessions received from powerful people will not be confused with compromise.

Parent Partnership

A group that is often in need of expert partnership is parents of disabled children. These parents face numerous situations that require specialized skills or knowledge. Consultants interested in advocacy can be helpful by supplying parents with information concerning new developments in law and suggesting ways to navigate the somewhat confusing service delivery network.

Mental health professionals and educators rarely study macrosystem change, therefore it has been discussed at length in this chapter. It is important to remember, however, that being an advocate for system change is a difficult task, requiring tireless energy and commitment to values and goals. It is important not to glamorize the excitement associated with the righteous David (you!) taking on the evil Goliath (dehumanizing systems). The work is difficult, alienation from others is always a threat, and the tangible rewards are meager. People with a reputation for challenging the system may have difficulty finding a job. Most employers prefer team players. Although team players sometimes decrease the effectiveness of an organization (e.g., the "group think" attributed to the Lyndon B. Johnson Cabinet during the Vietnam War), most people in a system value its regularities and resist efforts at change.

DO WE KNOW ENOUGH?

The skills associated with each consultation target and operational level are designed to provide the consultant with some basic tools for facilitating change. All of these strategies deserve further study and investigation. What seems clear is that in a world as complex and pluralistic as ours, dogmatic adherence to any one approach is foolish and ineffective.

SUMMARY

The operational levels and change targets a consultant chooses reflect his or her skills. Although many consultation skills are generic, others are appropriately used under specific circumstances. For example, effectively countering irrational thinking on the part of the consultee (i.e., theme interference) requires approaches that are accomplished at a microsystem level; that is, an individual consultant working with a single consultee. In contrast, consultants who wish to engage in macrosystem change must become adept at organizing constituencies, well informed about legal remedies for problem situations, and facile at understanding the power relationships within schools.

SUGGESTED READINGS

Dixon, D. N., & Glover, J. A. (1984). *Counseling: A problem solving approach.* New York: John Wiley & Sons.

Elliott, S. N., & Witt, J. C. (Eds.). (1986). *The delivery of psychological services in schools: Concepts, processes, and issues.* Hillsdale, NJ: Lawrence Erlbaum Associates.

Idol, L., & West, J. F. (1987). Consultation in special education: Part II. Training and practice. *Journal of Learning Disabilities, 20,* 474–494.

Maitland, R. E., Fine, M. J., & Tracy, D. B. (1985). The effects of an interpersonally based problem solving process on consultation outcome. *Journal of School Psychology, 23,* 337–345.

Mearig, J. (1974). On becoming a child advocate in school psychology. *Journal of School Psychology, 2,* 121–129.

Norris, D. A., Burke, J. P., & Speer, A. L. (1990). Tri-level service delivery: An alternative consultation model. *School Psychology Quarterly, 5,* 89–110.

Chapter 4

How to Enter and When to Stay

Knowing how to consult does not guarantee an opportunity to do it. The tremendous press in most organizations for direct service interferes with the implementation and maintenance of a consultation program. In addition, even the person who has been invited into an organization to be a consultant may find his or her efforts frustrated. The problem of successfully introducing consultation to an organization from an internal or external base is the entry problem.

Entry refers, therefore, to both the arrival of a consultant into a system and to the expansion of services within a system. (Refer to Figures 4.1 and 4.2 for a graphic representation of the problem.) Interestingly, the issues concerned with the dual aspects of entry are similar. That is, the groundwork, observation, and conceptualizations needed to accomplish physical entry are necessary again when new services, new people, or new problems become part of the consultation effort.

A consultation entry from an external base is described first in this chapter, followed by a discussion of consultation entry from an internal point. Issues associated with contracts, organizational assessment, confidentiality, entry failure, and the choice of other than consultation services for an organization are also discussed. Consultants must be able to specify the following if consultation service is to be successful in an organization:

1. Assess personal skills and history of change efforts in the organization before agreeing to consultation.
2. Specify the amount of time, effort, and money that may be expended and if the consultation will be cost-effective.
3. Be aware of different theories of change in terms of targeting

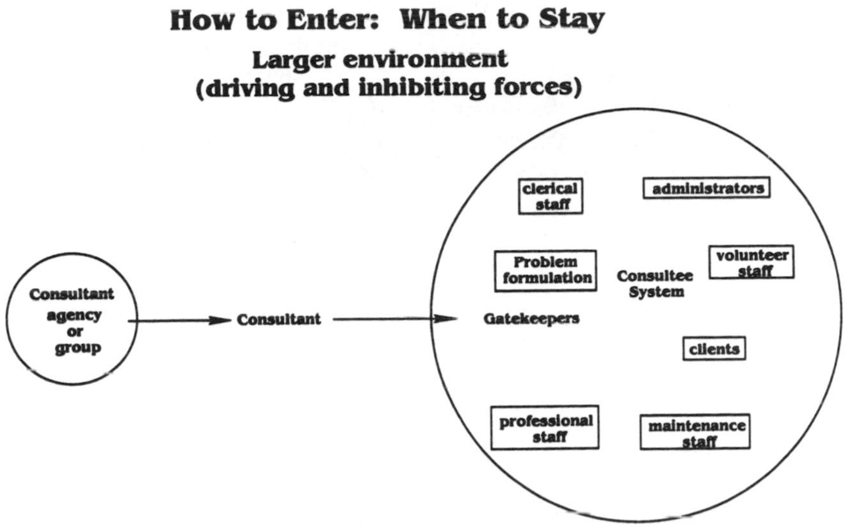

How to Enter: When to Stay

Larger environment
(driving and inhibiting forces)

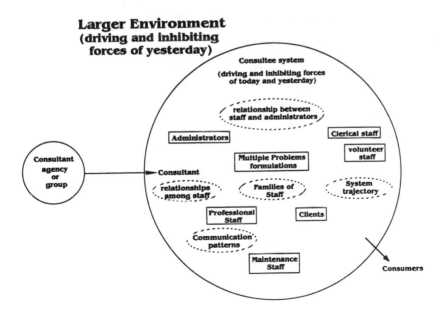

FIGURE 4.1. The Initial Entry Problem: Crossing the Organizational Boundary

Larger Environment
(driving and inhibiting
forces of yesterday)

FIGURE 4.2. The Continuing Entry Problem: Identifying Top Priority Problems

consultation problems (e.g., grass-roots vs. top-level work, crisis situations vs. prevention, affective vs. cognitive strategies).

4. Establish a written or verbal contract with the consultee, stating areas of responsibility and topics that will be covered.

5. Make long-range plans, viewing change as a sequential process aimed at preventing system dysfunction rather than merely remediating current problems.

6. Be clear regarding the target and operational levels of consultation. Know who the consultee and client are.

7. Recognize the potential complexity of the relationship between the consultant and the consultee, including issues of dependency, authority, confidentiality, and competence.

EXTERNALLY BASED CONSULTANTS

Many organizations use external consultants. Well-known experts, professional consultants, and university professors are likely to be recruited. These people may also promote themselves as potentially useful through letters, brochures, telephone contacts, and so on. Most federally funded projects have monies earmarked for consultant use during planning, implementation, and evaluation.

Despite the proliferation of the use of consultants, few organizations understand what services should be expected of consultants. Most problem formulations that trigger a consultation request are either vague and diffuse (e.g., staff has low morale) or specific (e.g., staff needs training in a new therapy technique). Consultants often find that the host organization does not know what to do about a particular issue and is not sure what the problem is.

The crucial challenge facing external consultants is the ability to make a quick and accurate assessment of what is troubling an organization. There is pressure for some immediate assessment because consultants must provide a description of what their services will look like, how long they will work, what people they need to talk with, and the probability of success.

Such information is reasonable to expect from a consultant but requires the consultant to do some preliminary and realistic assessments. The consultant may be tempted to leap into consultation before looking into the realities of the host system.

On the other hand, sometimes consultants attempt entry into an organization because they are committed to the organization's improvement. A consultant can have an ideology that supports intervention even when the probabilities for success are unknown. Examples include some school consultations, mental health department to community agency consultations, and consultations established for training purposes. In cases like these, organizational assessments are invaluable but are not usually used to eliminate consultation sites, rather to enhance the chances for a successful consultation.

Seymour Sarason's Port of Entry speech is an eloquent example of how such ideologically based consultants might describe their consultation plans.

> What do we propose to do? It is easier for me to tell you what we do not intend to do. For one thing, we do not intend to come into a school in order to see how many problem children we can refer out to various agencies. There is no doubt that you know a lot of children who should utilize the services of a child-guidance clinic or family service society. To come in with the intent of referring them out is both unfair and unrealistic because these agencies, particularly the child-guidance clinics, are overwhelmed with cases and generally have long waiting lines. Even if the child-guidance clinic could take the child on, it would take them quite a while to get to first base with the child and in the meantime you still have that child in your class. Treatment procedures are neither that quick nor effective, to allow you to expect that your difficulties with the child are over once you know he is being seen in a clinic. The question we have asked of ourselves is how can we be of help to the teacher in the here and now with whatever questions and problems she raises with us. In short, we want to see how we can be of help within the confines of the school. It is not our purpose to come into a school to sit and talk to teachers, however helpful and interesting that might be. . . . For example, it is in our experience of no particular help to a teacher to be told that a child needs individual attention, a need which differentiates him not at all from the rest of us. What a teacher wants to know is when, how, and for what goals the "individual attention" will occur, and this requires a first-hand knowledge of what is going on. . . . We are not the experts who can come up with solutions even though we have no first-hand knowledge of the context in which the problem has been identified. We have no special strength or power except that which flows from our being able to establish a situation of mutual trust between teachers and ourselves. To the extent that we can demonstrate to you by our manner, gesture, and verbalization that we want to help, is to the extent we made the development of this mutual trust more likely and quickly to occur. There is one aspect of the way we function that I think needs some elaboration. I have already told you why it is essential for us, if our efforts are to be maximally useful, that we spend time in the classroom. Another reason this is essential resides in the one advantage we have over the teacher (i.e., we do not have the awesome responsibility of having to handle a large group of young characters five days a week for several hours each day), a responsibility that makes dispassionate observation and clear thinking extraordinarily difficult. We can enjoy the luxury of being in the classroom without the responsibility of the teacher for managing and thinking about 25 or more unique personalities. We do not envy you, although I am quite sure that you will envy us for not having your responsibilities. It is precisely because we are "free" that we can observe

what is going on in a way not usually possible for a teacher. . . . We do not
know to what extent we can be of help to you. We do not present ourselves
as experts who have answers. We have much to learn about this helping
process. If our previous work with teachers is any guide, the type of service
we want to develop is one that they feel they need. The only thing we can
guarantee you is that we want to learn and to help. We have much to learn
from you, and together we may be able to be of help to children in school.
(Sarason et al., 1960, pp. 58–62)

Research suggests that introductions such as the foregoing result in increased and more appropriate requests for service (Chandy, 1974).

Logistics of Service

In addition to assessing the feasibility of consultation and describing
their planned activities, external consultants must specify the details of
their involvement with an organization. For example, fee, expenses, and
time reserved for consultation should be stated clearly. The amounts that
consultants charge vary according to their areas of expertise and their
renown. Fees should be set with careful observance of professional codes
of ethics. The American Psychological Association (APA) code specifies
that professionals may not take part in fee fixing or fee splitting and that
a portion of a professional's time should be reserved for pro bono services.
Although these guidelines were written with the client-psychologist relationship in mind, their spirit should be observed in consultation endeavors
as well.

Whatever the charge, there should be no ambiguity concerning all of the
consultant's reimbursements and obligations. Consultants often work in
organizations that suffer from a lack of clear goal setting and communication skills. At the least, consultants can model clarity in their negotiations
with consultees.

Mental health personnel may find financial dealings crass, and thus fail
to delineate financial aspects of the consultation. Such failure usually
results in discomfort for both consultant and consultee.

Time spent doing consultation also requires clarification. Are the consultants to be paid only for the hours they spend at the site? Or can
planning and development be reimbursed as well? Such an understanding
is necessary before a per-hour or daily, on-site charge can be fixed. One
3-day consultation involved three separate training sessions along with
administrator and teacher consultations. At least 3 days of work were
involved in preparing for the training sessions. Most organizations will
anticipate additional or higher fees for situations such as this.

Consultants should let people know when they will be on site. Preplanned schedules should be followed exactly. This makes it easier for consultees to locate and schedule time with the consultant, creates a sense of predictability in the consultant's behavior, and may increase consultee use of consultation.

Many administrators are enraged by tardiness and absenteeism among their employees. For some, the concern to have everyone present borders on an obsession. Consultants should be aware of behavior that typically upsets administrators.

> *Case Example.* While chatting with a rather authoritarian principal in the hallway of a school, a consultant witnessed the following scene. A teacher entered the building 2 minutes past the first bell and hurried to her classroom. The principal watched her until just before she turned a corner. At that moment he bellowed, "It's about time you joined us, Mrs. Curtis!"
>
> Children and other teachers in the area fell silent, and the rebuked teacher hung her head and dashed away to her room. After a dramatic moment of silence, the principal said loudly to the consultant, "This is going into her file right now!" He stalked away.

The foregoing example illustrates a number of concerns relative to the authoritarian school principal. Rules are rules for this principal, and a consultant's successful entry may depend on conscientious adherence to small details.

External consultants make mistakes more frequently than internals in terms of breaking a system's unwritten rules. Such errors are usually helpful diagnostically but are disconcerting when they occur, both for the consultant and the consultees.

One rule that is easy to break is the who-talks-to-whom rule. Consultants who assume that everyone knows their role and that all organizational members are potential consultees are sometimes rudely awakened and should ask before talking. They should tell the contact consultee what their typical interviewing or surveying needs are and see what reaction is elicited. In addition, it is good form to ask for a list of people who are not intended for any consultation contact. There may be no such list. In any event, the consultant learns important data concerning the consultees and reduces the chance of marring the consultation work.

> *Case Example.* An assistant principal of an elementary school angrily told a new consultant that all information given to teachers must be approved by her before it was distributed. The consultant had shared some handouts regarding special education placement rules with the general education staff in response to some of the new teachers' confusion over referral steps. The assistant principal was serious that no information was to be given to teachers without her direct approval.

INTERNALLY BASED CONSULTANTS

Internal consultants are present in an organization and may have been hired to be consultants or to provide other services. An example of the first type of internal consultant would be a behavior management consultant retained by a school to assist teachers. School psychologists and resource teachers are examples of the second type. These professionals occupy other roles in the school system while providing consultation services.

Advantages and Disadvantages

Internal consultants require all the same skills as externals but have certain advantages and disadvantages when planning a consultation program. The advantages include the following:

1. A more thorough knowledge of the host system, facilitating accurate problem identification and reducing system-jarring errors; and
2. An established rapport with consultees.

Disadvantages associated with internal consultation include the following:

1. A tendency to see problems as do other members of the system because of the organizational acculturation that takes place in every group;
2. A somewhat diminished status (in contrast to externals) because of familiarity between the consultant and consultees; and
3. Potential difficulty in establishing new role dimensions in addition to the current role, including both new consulting functions (e.g., survey research) and new stresses on confidential relationships.

It is impossible to generalize about when internal versus external consultants are preferred. The context of the problem and organization and qualities of the people involved as potential consultees and consultants all influence decisions about the type and implentation of consultation.

Some research suggests that internal consultants who are somewhat marginal to their host organizations may be the most helpful (Browne, Cotton, & Golembiewski, 1977). Marginality refers to an emotional distance from and neutrality to the organization. Such an attitude of disengagement may preserve the internal from some of the aforementioned disadvantages.

Pipes (1981) raised an interesting point that deserves reiteration and some expansion. An organization's predilection for using internal versus external consultants may be related to other important organizational qualities. Never seeking outside help might indicate (a) a high opinion of full-time staff, or (b) a paranoia concerning outsiders' influences. Always going outside the organization might indicate (a) a desire to renew the organization through the planned import of new ideas and talents, or (b) an attempt to avoid chronic conflictual issues by regularly hiring a consultant to be a scapegoat for failure. There are, or course, many other possible shades of meanings to these organizational behaviors. The important entry questions for the consultant are, "Why work on this problem now?" and "Why am I being asked to do it?" Table 4.1 lists questions a consultant should entertain when entering an organization.

Internal consultants will know the history of an organization's problems. Although this might limit their creativity, it makes them aware of people to be contacted, procedures to be modified, and special interest groups to be mobilized for support.

Sarason (1982) pointed out that few aspiring innovators have taken the time to learn the history of change in a particular organization. As in all other human endeavors, those consultants who do not know history are doomed to repeat it. Unfortunately, the history of meaningful change occurring in human service organizations is somewhat dismal. Americans' and American social scientists' ahistorical stance has been pointed out repeatedly (Levine & Levine, 1970; Sarason & Doris, 1979).

A working knowledge of an organization's critical past incidents gives the internal consultant a decisive advantage. The consultant can share such knowledge with the consultee through sophisticated questions about the organization. It is better for the consultant to ask questions that show an understanding of pressing issues than to state what he or she knows about the consultee. Reeling off information is likely to create paranoia rather

Table 4.1. Questions to Consider During the Entry Process

About the client	What is the shared history between this consultee and client? What is the level of crisis, and what are the consultee's expectations regarding consultation? How well trained as a consultee is this consultee?
In relation to the consultant	What does the consultant offer that appears useful to the consultee? Does the consultee lose status by interaction with the consultant? Can consultees support both their own agendas and those of the consultant? Does the consultee experience authority problems? Does the problem look like dependency, defensiveness, or apathy?
About the consultee's field	What is the tradition of this field with regard to the use of consultants and orientation toward problem solving, individual efficacy, or team membership? What are characteristics of the consultee's preservice training?
About other colleagues	What pressure exists for consultees not to change? How supportive of innovation are colleagues?

than a good impression. This is especially likely if the system is experiencing substantial stress and crisis.

> *Case Example.* In his initial meeting with a principal of an elementary school, the new school psychologist wove the following questions into this first conversation.
>
> * What is this school's history with forming faculty teams?
> * How have recent realignment of district boundaries affected the population of the school?
> * What is the faculty's experience of the new math curriculum that was adopted the previous year throughout the district?
> * What is the ratio of new and experienced staff? Are there themes of strengths and needs in either of those groups?
>
>   The consultant's obvious familiarity with issues that concern most principals was impressive to the administrator. The principal's answers were of help to the consultant in planning consultation targets and strategies.

The advantage the internal consultant has in knowing the subtle aspects of the presenting problem can be lost if the consultant has become strongly identified as a member of a staff faction. All organizations contain subgroupings that might be defined by their tasks, age, religious or philosophical convictions, ethnic group, values, status, competence, location in the building, or other ties of allegiance. Inherent in the process of grouping is an identification of some as in-group and some as out-group. If this were not so, groups could not exist.

Internal consultants are likely to have been so identified. This may reduce consultant effectiveness by limiting meaningful access to all factions. Particularly divisive organizations use a lot of organizational energy on intrasystem competition and tend to label every newcomer and old-timer as quickly and decisively as possible as a member of some known faction. When there are warring camps, each wants to know who is the comrade and who is the enemy.

This situation provides challenges to both external and internal consultants. On the one hand, an internal consultant might be seen as a spy for the other side. On the other hand, organizational factions may fight to gain the external consultant's approval, or the external consultant may unwittingly align with a group, thus reducing consultation effectiveness.

In chronically factionated systems at least some of the members derive satisfaction from the conflict.

> *Case Example.* The chairperson of a large academic department asked a consultant to investigate the sources of tremendous faculty unrest and low morale. Rumors, charges and countercharges, and ill will were pervasive. The faculty was ostensibly divided between researchers and nonresearchers. Superficial data gathering revealed, however, that such a descriptor did not accurately

classify members of each group. Rather, it appeared that there were three groups: oldtimers who had once been powerful (have-nots), oldtimers and newcomers who had always been or were now fairly uninvolved in the department and the controversies, and newcomers who had arrived with or shortly after the chairperson and were in positions of power (haves).

Valid data gathering was virtually impossible, as members of the have-not group used all interview time to check on the loyalties of the consultant and then extol their group's virtues while derogating the other groups. The relatively neutral group had stayed so by keeping their mouths, eyes, and ears shut, and so were only minimally helpful.

After 3 days of data gathering using several approaches, the consultant hypothesized that the have-nots enjoyed their role as critics of the system and had no energy or intention to resolve their differences with other department members. The chairperson was offered administrative coaching on the matter, but only minor organizational adjustments appeared possible.

Summary

Entry is a complex process that should not be taken for granted even when initial information from a system indicates how delighted everyone is with the consultant and the consultation program. In the same system, externally based versus internally based consultants may deal with markedly different problem presentations. There are advantages and disadvantages to either location and, in most cases, the consultation work can be done successfully from either base. Careful observation and data gathering about an organization's use of consultants in the past and historical response to problem solving are critical for eventual successful entry.

CONTRACTS

There is a substantial amount of literature concerning contracts in consultation (e.g., Gallessich, 1974; Martens, Lewandowski, & Houk, 1989; Pipes, 1981). A contract is a verbal or written agreement between the consultant and the consultee that specifies the parameters of the relationship including fees, obligations, times, acceptable activities, time limits, and so on. The consultant must remember the following points about contracts:

1. Whatever the form of the contract, its particulars must be clear.
2. In addition to whatever else the initial contract contains, it should also discuss renegotiation at the request of the consultant or consultee.

3. The contract should be negotiated with the person or people who
    have the power to see that its terms are carried out.

In the following example, the consultant has been at a school for 6
months but experiences marred entry with a new consultee.

Case Example. The consultant believed that her series of meetings with a new
consultee, a fourth-grade teacher, had gone well. Later the consultant heard
through another consultee that the fourth-grade teacher was dissatisfied
with the consultant for not being reliable. The areas of responsibility between teacher and consultant had been left ambiguous. The teacher had
expected some direct help with the troubling child. The consultant believed
responsibility for implementing the consultation plans belonged completely
with the consultee.

This is one example of the many mini-contracts consultants make continuously during the progress of their work. It is sometimes tempting to
let some of the details involved in a planned intervention go unclaimed by
either consultant or consultee. It may be that each hopes the other will take
responsibility for it, or simply that precise problem definition has not been
attained.

Another important aspect of the contract should be a procedure for
evaluation and change. This might be as simple as, "I'll check back with
you in 3 weeks to see if there are changes to be made." Or the clause might
be written in the contract specifying a meeting of all interested parties at
a certain time to assess and perhaps change the focus of the consultation.
This need for renegotiation is important in consultation because a well-
done consultation creates change and uncovers new information. Consultants learn more about organizations as their work progresses and may
completely reconceptualize the problem formulations. When that happens, the consultant may need sanction to perform different roles or activities. The renegotiation process also models feedback skills and the renewal
process each organization might be implementing to improve its task or
maintenance functions.

Finally, the obvious reason for making the contract with the legitimate
person deserves some elaboration. First, when negotiating for a consultation endeavor, it is important to talk with the people who will actually
decide when and if a consultant will be accepted. It is common for decision
makers to have scouts in the field who suggest potential consultants. It is
fine to have a first round of negotiations with such scouts, but consultants
should not feel certain that they have been hired until they speak with the
decision maker.

Another aspect of this issue involves determining who the consultee is.
Consultants are often hired by administrators to consult with staff mem-

bers. The consultant must have a go-ahead from the administrator but cannot consider entry complete until a relationship has been established with each of the consultees. In this situation, the consultant is well advised to arrange regular meeting times with the administrator to investigate the need for administrative consultation. Change, elusive as it is, proceeds more smoothly from the top down.

If the consultee organization does not have a formal contractual agreement procedure (many just ask the consultant to sign a purchase order including his or her Social Security number), the consultant can simply write the agency a letter after the decision to begin consultation has been made. The letter should restate all the particulars and ask for a reply if there are points in need of clarification.

Internal consultants must gain the support of their supervisors as they begin consultation efforts. Gaining this support may demand imagination on the part of the consultant. The consultant must show how the new interventions will fit with other approaches in reaching the organization's continuing goals. The most persuasive argument often revolves around a more efficient means of carrying out the old roles and tasks, thereby affording time for new projects.

It is important to note the difference between goals and intervention strategies. The consultant's professional judgment about intervention strategies is valuable to organizations. Goal setting is in the policy realm of the employing organization. Consultants may give helpful input regarding goals but must understand that each organization has some particular mission. Part of a consultant's job is the ability to determine what intervention skills to use for reaching certain goals. If the job defines the techniques, the consultant becomes merely a technician.

In some schools the exact assessment and intervention strategies to be used by staff are prescribed by people outside the working profession. Obviously, membership in an organization requires an openness to compromise and negotiation, but professionals must stay in charge of their practice and not allow others to dictate what the best practices are. The responsibility involved in this privilege is, of course, that professionals must stay abreast of the most current and best practices available.

The internal consultant must gain the commitment of the supervisor to the consultation project and should anticipate decreasing supervisory support as soon as pressure for traditional service delivery increases. The consultant should be prepared for loss of support with careful documentation of the positive effects of the consultation project and should collect data continuously and make it available to decision makers. Internal consultants must consider the constant education of the organization as part of their contract.

ORGANIZATIONAL ASSESSMENT

The organizational assessment task is substantial. There are many important sources of information regarding this process (e.g., Argyris, 1971; Bennis, 1969; Blake & Mouton, 1976, 1978; Cummings, 1980; French & Bell, 1978; Katz & Kahn, 1978; Lawrence & Lorsch, 1969; Schein, 1969; Schmuck, Runkel, Saturen, Martell & Derr, 1972; Secord & Backman, 1974; Steele, 1973). The following sections provide some basic guidelines for performing assessment to maximize consultation entry success. The guidelines are also helpful in planning consultation interventions throughout the duration of consultation work. There is always new information to be learned about an organization. An openness to such information will enhance consultation and serve as a check on initial observation.

Rationales for Organizational Assessment

Traditionally, assessment has meant a focus on micro aspects of the person (e.g., personality traits, intellectual skills, vocational aptitudes). There is, however, a growing body of assessment conceptualizations that focus on more macro units (e.g., families, small groups, entire organizations). Perhaps Lewin's (1951) conceptualizations of life space are the precursors to macro assessment (Barker, 1978; Barker & Gump, 1964; Gallessich, 1973; Kounin, 1970; Olson, Russell, & Sprenkle, 1983; Patterson, Reid, Jones, & Conger, 1975; Sarason, 1981; Sarason & Doris, 1979; Schein, 1969; Schmuck, 1976; von Bertalanffy, 1968).

The targets of interest in an organizational assessment are not the individuals, intrapsychic lives of the individuals, or even the behaviors of the individuals per se who compose the organizations. Rather, behavioral regularities (Sarason, 1981) are extracted from observations. Norms; communication patterns; leadership emergence and style; decision-making procedures; uses of time and space; interdependence, cooperation, and competition among subsystems; and social and emotional climate are a few of the areas to be scrutinized.

Organizational assessment has three primary purposes during entry:

1. Understand the organization according to important systemic variables.
2. Understand the influence of these variables on the behaviors of organization members.
3. Design and implement strategies to accomplish consultation contract goals.

Organizational variables affect individual behavior. In fact, organizational regularities may override personal variables. Consider how during parent-teacher meetings parents enter classrooms and know they should sit in the pupils' desks and await the arrival of a teacher. Upon entering the school organization, they shift their behaviors (many are themselves teachers or other professionals) to match what they understand to be the demands of the organization.

Important Organizational Dimensions

Several major areas of an organization must be examined to accomplish an assessment. Each area contains a number of important components. Consultants should consider the attributes of effective organizations rather than looking only for problems. Characteristics of healthy systems include (a) appropriately autonomous staff; (b) many opportunities for self-development; (c) sense of belonging to organization; (d) recognition of successful employees; (e) jobs that are attractive, interesting, and satisfying; (f) goals that are clear, challenging, attainable, and attractive; (g) provision of resources; (h) elimination of constraints to performance; and (i) interpersonal and group processes that support goal attainment.

Physical Factors. The physical plant(s) of the organization can be examined to ascertain the amount of usable equipment that is available. This includes machinery and office supplies. The maintenance of the equipment and of the facility itself are important. Other important aspects of the physical environment include the existence and quality of staff lounges, the design of the reception area, and the artwork that adorns the halls and offices. It is also possible to make note of the physical marks of status within a system. Such things as paintings on the walls, rugs on the floor, corner offices, drapes, and wooden versus metal desks are often associated with power within a system (Steele, 1973).

The entering consultant can form hypotheses about how a particular building or subsystem ranks in the larger system by seeing how clean and well equipped the facility is. Physical dimensions of the staff lounge (e.g., comfortable furniture, convenient location, coffee available, etc.) may shed light on the concern administrators show for the comfort of their staff and/or how much the staff values each other.

The office or area reserved for greeting or screening outsiders may be an important area to study and experience. This area may represent psychological as well as physical entry into a building. Is it comfortably furnished? Are there magazines or brochures in the area? Is the room physically arranged so that newcomers are recognized immediately?

Consultants who are waiting to be received by the consultee should observe how others who enter are received. Are there differences based on some obvious dimensions such as age, race, or role (e.g., parent vs. school board trustee)? The consultant should also notice if staff tends to drop by this room for quick chats or just to relax for a moment.

Social and Emotional Climate. As soon as consultants gain some physical access to a building (e.g., the administrator conducts a tour), they should note how the staff seems to relate to one another. Does their conversation seem warm, task oriented, stilted, or only social? Later, consultants can ascertain if the staff tends to work as a whole faculty on problems or in small groups, and which staff (if any) socializes outside of work.

In addition, the quality of the vertical relationships should be conceptualized: Does the administrator do personal favors for the staff? Does staff share personal concerns with the administrator? Is the administrator first to work and last to leave? How accessible is the administrator? The use of written versus face-to-face communication is important to notice. Heavy reliance on written memos may reflect a formal, rigid organizational structure. Face-to-face feedback concerning poor performance is important. The exclusive use of written memos in this area may indicate an administrator who has difficulty giving feedback in constructive, nonpunitive ways.

Another indication of the social and emotional climate of an organization is the way in which weak members are treated. For example, new, sick, or recently bereaved staff members are at least temporarily vulnerable. Are they offered guidance or support? How does the organization respond—as a whole, in small groups, or individually? Are there procedures in place to support vulnerable members, or is every incident a new problem to solve?

Finally, the culture and norms of the organization must be analyzed. Analyses of organizational culture are available (e.g., Sarason's *The Culture of the School and the Problem of Change* [1982]). Each organization has unique features, so it is important to be open to new possibilities. An organizational culture is made up of many spoken and unspoken rules, habits, attitudes, beliefs, and preferences. Dress, what is discussed, what is not discussed, punctuality parameters, quality of humor (e.g., wit vs. sarcasm), attendance at meetings, and quality and quantity of staff meetings are all contributors to an organizational culture.

Power. Power is a critical variable to investigate during entry and for the organizational assessment. It is important to ascertain who are the haves and the have-nots and what is the major dimension that accrues power. Power may be associated with legitimate structures within the organization (e.g., bosses); it may be due to competence or seniority; it may have been delegated to an individual; and it may be built on the allegiance of others or due to connections with others. Powerful people can be identified by observing to whom verbalizations are directed at meetings, whose opinions are sought and who initiates the most at meetings, or who is the most successful in getting a policy adopted.

Consultants must also note the way power is used. For example, some people with power may be fearful of using it and alienating people. Many people who need to act decisively and authoritatively simply do not. Others are so concerned about losing any gram of influence that they allow no participation in decision making and block the dissemination of important information.

> *Case Example.* The principal of a large high school had an iron grip on the faculty. No one was hired, given keys, tenured, and so on, without his direct and absolute involvement. He would even stop simple maintenance tasks (e.g., fixing a window) that he had not directly approved. He would not make information concerning work loads or assignments public, so everyone worked in a vacuum of information, never knowing if they were doing enough. Years later and long after this principal's retirement, when a consultant visited the school, he was struck by the low level of faculty involvement in decision making. The faculty, however, felt that they had made significant strides toward decentralization and were satisfied.

Because consultants are interested in facilitating change, they must understand the power realities of each new consultee organization. Change is easier to accomplish with the support of those who are already influential. Martin (1978) described consultants as having expert and referent power. So, too, do consultees. The relationships among those with power in an organization are important to discern. One simple strategy is to draw or obtain an organizational chart. Sketching the formal lines of authority may suggest the site of a particular problem. People with informal (or referent) power can also be added to an organizational chart to highlight other strengths or problem areas.

Administrative Style. Administrative style is closely related to power. Consultants must be able to detail the way in which administrators handle their work. There are extremes in administrative styles—from those who delegate every task and decision, to those who refuse any input. Most administrators fall between these two extremes.

The consultant must match the style of the administrator during entry. For example, if the administrator is controlling, consultants should appear regularly with progress reports and make sure the administrator knows their arrival and departure times and is informed as to who they are consulting.

The consultant may also want to offer consultation to the administrator and so should be able to formulate some goals for administrative consultation. Consultants in this situation may scan the system for dysfunction related to the controlling style of the leader. If none is found, then no administrative consultation is indicated. If issues of autonomy, low creative output, or anxiety are present, then the consultant might begin a program of consultation aimed at increasing the administrator's tolerance for ambiguity and openness to decentralized decision making.

Leadership is a fascinating and important scholarly area, and it is helpful for consultants to develop expertise about it. The most sophisticated understanding of leadership considers characteristics of followers, tasks to be accomplished, and other contextual demands when developing a profile of an effective leader. There are no pat formulas in terms of the amount of participation in decision making, delegation, concern with task accomplishment, concern with human needs, or interpersonal style.

Other factors associated with administrative style that the consultant should investigate are the reward system (e.g., is it congruent with stated objectives?); the administrator's theory about people (i.e., people are innately good or innately bad); the administrator's commitment to the staff (or is this job just a stepping stone?); the administrator's attitude toward the client population (supportive and caring vs. punitive and blaming); and the administrator's attitude toward the consultant (facilitator vs. pipeline or spy). All of this information affects the consultation effort. Its relevance may not be immediately obvious, but the knowledge enhances the consultant's chances for successful interventions.

Health of the Organization. The final dimension to consider in organizational assessment is the overall health of the organization. Every level of the organization should be considered along with processes that are known to create difficulties.

Scapegoating is a sign of an organization in distress. It refers to a process by which all organizational or personal problems or weaknesses are blamed on some other system, process, or person. For example, teachers' difficulties with children are blamed on intractable home situations, thus relieving the teacher of the responsibility to make attempts to help a child. Pervasive scapegoating perpetuates irresponsibility among consultees and decreases the number of alternatives to which they are open.

Another systematic indicator to monitor is integration among subsystems. Cooperative, coordinated action among and between subsystems is often vital if system goals are to be realized. Consultants must observe interface interactions (i.e., transactions between different subgroups) to determine the quality of the integration. The needs for integration of subsystem efforts vary across organizations. Some organizations are composed of working groups that are independent of each other while other organizations depend on close coordination among groups. Even with these differences in mind, however, consultants often observe competition, territoriality, expansionism, and scapegoating. Some administrators believe the system is improved by competition across the subsystems. Mild competition can be an enhancer, but often competition becomes the focus.

Case Example. As the declining birth rate in the early 1980s affected urban centers, some elementary schools were closed. It was the principals' job to make sure their schools seemed irreplaceable in the district configuration.

The comparisons became heated, however, with trivial differences in floor plans becoming major items of discussion. The teaching staffs were thrown into comparisons of each other's degrees, experience, evaluations, and relationships with parents. The result was a marked decline in morale, even in schools not currently faced with closing.

Related to the integration of subsystems is the permeability or rigidity of the organizational boundary to the environment. The relative openness of a particular organization to other community systems should not be static. Permeability should vary according to intrasystem development and particular issues. For example, early in an organization's development it might be open and inviting of new input. Following this phase, it may shut out new input for awhile in the hopes of testing what has been accomplished thus far. Similarly, an organization may allow open information exchange about some matters but be rigid in relation to others (e.g., client or staff personnel files).

The consultant must look for strengths and deficits along this boundary and identify the gate keepers of the boundaries. Some organizations lack skills in making themselves known or involving others in their functioning. Others have to be supported to open their doors to input they have labeled as adversarial, unsympathetic, or undermining.

A willingness to entertain new ideas and differences is crucial to viability. Rigid systems are in danger of an organizational leveling or entropy because nothing new or challenging is imported. What they contribute to the larger environment may become obsolete or irrelevant if there is no regular monitoring process of the larger environment's needs or new priorities.

Role clarity is another aspect of organizational functioning. Do people know what is expected of them and what to expect from others? Such shared understandings are imperative. Roles may be so clear that they are rigid, or so diffuse that they are invisible. Flexibility is optimal when people are free to change parts of their job descriptions to meet current interests or organizational needs. People should be willing to do what they can to achieve organizational goals and be allowed to be different from one another in that pursuit. Consultants might notice attitudes such as "It's not my job" or frustration because people do not know to whom to turn for advice or action.

Clarity of and agreement on goals should also be investigated. Sometimes an organization's stated goals are contradictory. For example, notice the discrepancy between "promote curious, independent thinking among children" compared with classroom realities that demand conformity and rarely give children encouragement or time to ask questions. Consultants must ascertain what the real goals are and the discrepancies between goals and actual behaviors.

Another aspect of organizational health concerns problem-solving patterns. Does the organization avoid confronting problems, overdiscuss issues, or squarely face problems and develop action plans? What decision-making style is used: voting, minority rule, administrative fiat, consensus, or unanimity? Each of these has costs and benefits. The consultant must decide if the benefits outweigh the costs. If they do not, some coaching on decision-making procedures may be in order. The consultant must also consider if the latent resources of the organization are brought to bear on problems and important decisions. Many organizations always seek outside consultation and never use or discover what is already present in the organization. If this is a problem, a consultant can direct and redirect planners toward existing resources in terms of people, publications, experience, procedures, or equipment.

Gallessich (1974) mentioned the trajectory of the organization as important organizational data. Is the organization's immediate environment on an upswing or downswing? Many teachers have been faced with dramatic changes in student bodies. Students and families that were close to the teachers' backgrounds and culture have been replaced by poor minority students in urban ghettos. Teachers may need support to try new teaching strategies to meet new challenges. This level of energy may differ from the energy of teachers at a new school, showered with new programs, and supported by well-educated parents and well-prepared students.

The final and perhaps most important question that the consultant must ask is, "Can this organization balance stability with change?" Every organization must be adaptable to change, facing up to what is happening inside and outside. Many organizations avoid self-analysis. Renewal and viability depend, however, on an organization's willingness to examine itself, hold steady where possible, and change where needed. If there is sign of decline (e.g., reduced enrollment at a university), the consultant might investigate the organization's procedures for self-analysis and correction. If these are lacking, then the facilitation of such strategies is an important consultation goal.

Case Example. A high school had experienced several complaints regarding sexual harassment of students by faculty. An externally mandated self-study was initiated. The chairperson and members of the committee were untenured. None were given release time to accomplish the work. A representative from the district office chided the administration for discouraging meaningful criticism, especially during this period when there was an obvious need for some honest analyses of the concerns facing the student body.

Putting It Together

When all these observations have been made, the consultant is in a position to identify the following:

1. The organization's coping strengths and latent resources;
2. Areas of organizational difficulty; and
3. Obstacles to success.

These generalizations should be drawn from the assessment and be tested again when new data become available. In addition to careful observation, consultants can make use of system publications, local news, school journals, the organization's library, and existing charters or mission statements.

HOW TO FAIL

It may be helpful to refer back to chapter 2 and to read the comments by Rae-Grant (1972). The behaviors discussed there will interfere with successful entry as well as the successful maintenance of a consultation program. The following will also prevent successful consultation:

1. Ignore the norms of the organization. Use phones without asking, be late or unreliable, and dress in whatever fashion you feel comfortable.
2. Talk with one consultee about another or report to administrators about staff behaviors.
3. Wait in your office to be approached for service.
4. Criticize the system whenever possible to insiders and outsiders.
5. Fail to build a relationship with the top administrator.
6. Appear somewhat aloof and formal. Do not ask consultees any questions about who they are. Rather, spend time describing your own life and accomplishments.
7. Depend on administrator support to structure your activities. Insist on meeting with him or her frequently.
8. Announce your intention to engage in activities that fit only your interests and your agendas.

Although we have not tested each of these guidelines empirically, we feel sure of their efficacy.

WHEN NOT TO OFFER
CONSULTATION

A well-done organizational assessment is used to decide on the feasibility of consultation as well as to provide diagnostic information on consultation targets and operational levels. It is difficult to provide absolute guidelines to abort an entry or discontinue consultation. Some signals at entry that may predict an unsuccessful effort include (a) autocratic or unsupportive administrators, (b) an organization in extreme crisis, and (c) an organization with an overwhelming need for direct services.

Consultation is not a panacea and is best used when it matches the situation. If there are many children in a school that arrive daily hungry, tired, or abused, the consultant's time might be better used doing advocacy for those children at local welfare agencies rather than offering teachers mental health or behavioral consultation. It is possible, of course, that helping teachers succeed with the children might be a powerful form of advocacy.

Sometimes the assessment shows a need for consultation, but not the type the consultant offers. The consultant should consider the following list of interventions. Some professional honesty and humility are in order when examining this list. Few, if any, consultants are equally well qualified in all interventions.

1. *Diagnosis:* interviews, questionnaires, surveys, meetings, observation, archival data.
2. *Team building:* getting jobs done, skills to accomplish tasks, relationships among team members, leader skills.
3. *Intergroup activities:* joint work with the output as a single organization.
4. *Education and training:* improve skills, abilities, knowledge in leadership, responsibilities and functions of group members, decision making, goal setting and planning, problem solving, technology.
5. *Structural activities:* job enrichment, communication patterns, supervisory patterns.
6. *Mediation:* confrontation, conflict management.
7. *Coaching:* feedback, exploration of alternative behaviors.
8. *Technological:* assist in determining best-fit technology for organization.

The organization might be well served by a curriculum expert, information flow analyst, or equipment expert. In this case, the consultant should facilitate a connection between the organization and the best resource for the situation. Private practitioners may find this directive difficult to follow. They may feel the economic pressure to accept all consultation offers. Our experience has indicated that such referrals are, however, well received by consultee systems and result in goodwill, good public relations, and requests for appropriate services at later dates.

When the interests or time available from the consultant do not match organizational needs, entry should not be completed and consultation should not be offered. Many consultants have accepted jobs that did not match their primary skills or interests and then found it hard to devote the appropriate time to the work. Or they might have simply taken on too much work. Mediocre or poorly done work usually results.

No one benefits if the consultant takes on too much work: The organization receives poor-quality service and the consultant becomes known for delivering poor-quality service. It is hard to say no, but it is best to examine each request and choose only those in which you are interested, for which you have appropriate time resources, and which have some chance for success.

Finally, consultants should not enter organizations with hidden personal agendas based on ideologies that run counter to the consultee organization. Although consultation is meant to engender change, it should support the best of the organization's values. Consultants may find themselves in value disagreements with an organization but may still feel committed to the overall goals of a group. Consultants should not enter an organization if they are not in agreement with the organization's public goals. Consultants should also beware of consulting with organizations that have personal meaning to them, positive or negative. Consultants who had a negative experience in parochial schools and blame it on a rigid, authoritarian church structure should not be parochial school consultants.

The key is for consultants to know themselves. They should be open to learning from others and seek advice on situations that arouse intense emotionality or tendencies to blame the consultee.

SUMMARY

Introducing consultation to an organization is a complex process that is affected by the position of the consultant—for example, is the consultant an external expert or an existing employee? Neither position guarantees success or failure, but each creates different challenges. To accomplish entry, the consultant must be adept at organizational assessment. This assessment approach demands that the consultant be able to observe important process events in an organization and understand the organization's regularities as well as the personalities of the consultees. Consultation failure is likely if mistakes are made during the entry process and if consultants offer consultation to organizations that are inappropriate targets.

SUGGESTED READINGS

Fuchs, D., & Fuchs, L. S. (1989). Exploring effective and efficient prereferral interventions: A component analysis of behavioral consultation. *School Psychology Review, 18,* 260–279.

Graden, J. L., Casey, A., & Christenson, S. L. (1985). Implementing a prereferral intervention system: Part 1. The Model. *Exceptional Children, 51,* 377–384.

Greshman, F. M. (1989). Assessment of treatment integrity in school consultation and prereferral intervention. *School Psychology Review, 18,* 37–50.

Gutkin, T. B., & Hickman, J. A. (1988). Teachers' perceptions of control over presenting problems and resulting preferences for consultation versus referral services. *Journal of School Psychology, 26,* 395–398.

Martens, B. K., Lewandowski, L. J., & Houk, J. L. (1989). The effects of entry information on the consultation process. *School Psychology Review, 18,* 225–234.

Chapter 5

Moving from Direct to Indirect Service Delivery

BARRIERS

A number of forces can inhibit the development of a consultation program (see Figure 5.1). The following are the most important of these forces:

1. The principal actors in the setting do not believe in the efficacy of consultation.
2. Appropriate training or practicum experiences have not been included in the professional socialization of the consultant.
3. The pressure for direct service is so great that there is no time to enlarge a direct service role to include indirect services.
4. The consulting role appears threatening to decision makers.

Each of these barriers to implementation deserves attention. Following a discussion of each, some strategies are discussed to accomplish the addition of consultation to a professional repertoire.

Does It Work?

Perhaps the greatest obstacle to good consultation is a pervasive belief among professionals (mental health personnel, resource room teachers, and so on) that they must be in direct remedial contact with "The Pathology." They are, after all, the ones who trained for years to treat complex problems. Two assumptions are operating here. One is that problems reside within clients. The second assumption is that consultation provides only a watered-down version of an intervention.

Where Is the Problem? A useful perspective in consultation practice is to recognize that problems are (a) organization difficulties, and (b) conceptu-

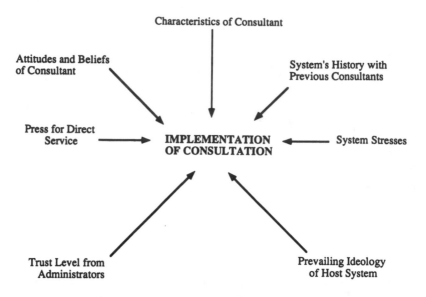

FIGURE 5.1. Forces Acting on the implementation of consultation.

alized in ways that interfere with their resolution. This perspective opens up several avenues of formulation for the consultant. First, he or she should look at how the identified problem is being maintained by the organization and, more subtly, how the problem is manifesting organizational difficulties. Such an analysis always suggests ways for the organization to change independent of client change.

Second, everyone has difficulties but only some of these become problems. The ones that become problems are not necessarily the most serious or difficult challenges. The problems are simply issues that require a different analysis, frame, or conceptualization. Like all other human perceptions, a problem has been constructed by the people involved. It can be reconstructed into a solution by changing the meaning attached to certain behaviors or changing the standards used to judge the event.

Case Example. Jason, a 14-year-old gifted youngster, had long hair, a quiet and reflective manner, and tended to make individualistic decisions regarding dress, interests, and behaviors. He was sensitive to others' feelings, especially in comparison to his cohorts.

His teachers were planning to remove him from the gifted curriculum because he had recently gotten a C in English and appeared to be sad and troubled at school. Investigation revealed that Jason liked his gifted classes and was not troubled by the C grade. He and his mother had a long history of emphasizing learning over grades as representing what was important at school. Further, his sadness at school was related not to academics but to some social isolation and some difficulties with his father, who had recently remarried.

With the help of the consultant, the teachers and Jason decided to maintain his academic program and seek some input for Jason regarding how to improve his social status and how to problem-solve with his father. An important element to these plans was a recognition that Jason's style may make it difficult for him to fit in to the junior high school culture. Jason was heartened to learn that he was in control of his peers' reactions to him and could choose to change or not.

Consultation Is Not Powerful Enough. Behavioral specialists may be frustrated to find that their plan is applied inconsistently. Humanistic practitioners might be put off by the evaluative structure of classrooms and the group focus of teachers. Neither of these consultants may trust others to implement intervention plans that meet their standards.

This barrier to a consultation program suggests that consultants must come to value others' efforts with children and simultaneously work to make their suggestions more palatable to consultees. Most of the available information comparing professional and nonprofessional helpers fails to find a clear advantage for the professional (e.g., Brickman et al., 1982; Cowen, 1982a; deCharms, 1976; Deci, Nezlek, & Sheinman, 1981; Hattie, Sharpley, & Rogers, 1984; Lepper & Greene, 1978; Tyler, Pargament, & Gatz, 1983). Most people who feel the need for help never approach a professional helper (Christensen, Birk, Brooks, & Sedlacek, 1976; Christensen & Magoon, 1974; Horwitz, 1978; McKinley, 1973). Some specialist humility is, therefore, in order.

If consultants can trust that involvement of consultees is necessary for improvement, they can devote time to increasing the acceptability of their suggestions, thus enhancing rather then supplanting the efforts of consultees. A further discussion of acceptability appears later in this chapter.

In summary, beliefs the consultant holds about the site of problem, the potential competence of other professionals, and professional territoriality all influence how successfully a consultation program can be introduced into a setting.

Role of Training

Many school psychology graduate programs offer some training in consultation. Consultation is rarely taught, however, to other branches of psychology, to special education, or in teacher training programs. This lack of training in consultation is an oversight given the clear need for adults in educational settings to use each other as resources (Conoley, 1989). Later in this chapter, prereferral or intervention assistance teams are discussed.

To be successful, all the members of such teams need training in consultation.

Some practitioners still hold consulting is a natural outgrowth of knowing something well. No formal course work is needed in consulting, only in what the consulting is about. Anyone who has tried to serve as an internal or external consultant to a system knows the inaccuracy of that analysis. It is not enough to know. Social influence is more complicated than content expertise.

Clinical Press

Even those who believe in consultation and have had appropriate training often have difficulty implementing consultation programs. The clinical press or pressure to do direct service is great in schools, mental health departments, and other human service agencies. These agencies often see direct service to a client group as their primary mission.

The clinical press problem cannot be overcome through individual intervention efforts. There are not enough trained specialists to meet children's needs by individual treatment. Organizational alternatives must be explored. One such alternative, prereferral teams (discussed later in this chapter), is a promising approach to dealing with barriers to consultation.

Consultation as a Threat

Ironic as it may seem, some decision makers view consultation or consultants as threats to their organizations. Administrative concern about the consultant is usually associated with fears the consultant will do the following:

1. Learn more about the organization than the administrator knows and discover weaknesses in the organization or administrator.
2. Waste the time of staff members by taking them away from regular client duties.
3. Align with malcontented staff members and facilitate unsanctioned change.

Successful consultation almost always depends on positive administrative backing. Organization development consultants know that they must gain approval from top administrators. Case-centered consultants may overlook this fact of organizational life and fail to give priority to activities aimed at building a positive relationship with top administrators.

Organization Knowledge. Administrators must value the contribution a consultant can make to an organization. They have a different perspective on organizational functioning than do staff members and may foresee a number of problems arising from a consultation effort. Decision makers deserve a careful description of how consultation works. They have a right to limit the scope of the consultant's work.

Consultants may find that stressed organizations do not welcome them. Although the organization may be in desperate need of additional input, the decision makers may feel that they cannot absorb any more change or disruption. In addition, autocratic administrators may demand such control over a consultative effort that there is no chance for success. Such administrators often cannot tolerate the idea that their staff is going to talk to an outsider over whom they have only limited control.

Consultants can assure administrators of their commitment to confidentiality and to positive change. They can explain that they will know the organization only from their own perspective—a perspective no more valid than any in operation. They can also remind administrators of consultants' ethical responsibilities to clients. In addition, consultants can promote consultation as a way to improve service to clients without expanding staff.

Protection of Staff. Consultants are often irritated at any but immediate, unconditional, positive regard from the top people in an organization. Such openness may actually be a danger signal. Administrative decision makers are charged with protecting the organization. Some interrogations and controls are signs of an administrator who is performing his or her role appropriately. Extreme openness may indicate a malfunction, with no one protecting the organization from outside inputs or assaults. On the other hand, extreme openness may indicate a positive history with previous consultants.

When the administrative control or suspicion concerning a consultant is an outgrowth of positive concern, it will abate as consultants prove themselves to be reliable and helpful to the organization. If the administrative concern is based on a general pattern of autocratic style and extreme needs for control, consultants must attempt to mitigate the administrator's fears. Consultants who work in such organizations must accommodate to administrative controls as nearly as possible until a consulting relationship can be developed with the administrator. When such a relationship is established, consultants can focus on changes in administrative style as a consultation target.

Unsanctioned Change. A quick way to be uninvited to a system is to engage in unsanctioned change efforts. Unsanctioned change involves the consultant in the following:

1. Hiding personal agendas for change;
2. Creating or exacerbating unrest among staff members;

3. Being genuinely available to only some of the people (or none of the people) in an organization; and

4. Failing to exhaust established change procedures before increasing internal or external stresses on an organization.

Consultants are hired to be advocates for a host organization. If this organization is not fulfilling its stated mission, it is part of the consultant's job to get the organization back on the right track. In most cases this involves collaboratively planned changes.

If an organization is still failing after a series of consultation activities of increasing directiveness, the consultant must seek advice from the organization and from a supervisor about other avenues to explore. The consultant is not empowered to introduce unwanted systemic change unless he or she has been dealing with clear ethical violations. A good supervisor and some clear personal values are needed to navigate through such a situation. Some of the issues are as follows:

1. How long does a consultant remain after unethical practices have been discovered? Part of the consultant's job is to be a correcting force in the organization. Consultants cannot leave an organization every time something goes wrong.

2. Are there ethical principles at stake or merely different political ideologies? Autocratic, graceless administrators may be bothersome, but are they hurting client services in a meaningful way? How are staff members implicated in supporting the autocracy of their supervisors?

3. Are seemingly quick, dramatic confrontations being planned to heighten consultant power and influence rather than facilitate change? Some people enjoy the excitement of conflict and intrigue as a lifestyle, not merely as a response to unbearable situational stress. Consultants must avoid overidentifying with such people in an organization.

4. A consultant should be able to take the role of others. Skills in conceptualizing each group's position are invaluable in developing a picture of how everyone in an organization contributes to both its successes and failures.

If they are talented, consultants balance vision and reality for organizations. A talented consultant is always able to offer a new way of considering a problem, an innovative idea, a style that helps others perform at a higher level.

BEYOND THE BARRIERS

Each of the concerns discussed as barriers to consultation is amenable to change. General suggestions are as follows:

1.   Seek training and self-development, especially in systemic under-standing of behavior and the practice and theory of human change.

2.   Establish professional support networks that serve a peer supervi-sory function to receive input on complex ethical and organizational issues. Supervisors are helpful in devising new ways to meet the clinical press and suggesting strategies to engage in long-range, preventive programming for an organization.

In addition to these guidelines, there are numerous specific behaviors to be aware of when moving from an exclusively direct service model to a consultation model (Conoley, Apter, & Conoley, 1981). For example, con-sultants should get to know consultees by establishing proximity to them. They should frequent consultee gathering places. They should schedule meetings with consultees to show interest in what they are doing and be sure the meetings conform to the norms of the organization in terms of time, place, and people present.

Consultants should focus attention on relationship building. They should take the time to ask enriching questions and then wait to hear the whole story. They should foster consultee self-respect by avoiding prema-ture judgments about them and by preventing them from looking foolish just because they do not know something. In addition, consultants should model calm problem solving during case discussions. This will reduce consultee anxiety without reducing their self-esteem. Consultees are anx-ious about consultants, so consultants should be ready for constant testing.

Consultants are role models to consultees. By modeling empathy, toler-ance for feelings, and a conviction that all human behavior is eventually understandable, consultants perform a valuable function within an organi-zation.

The services available through consultation must be clear to all those concerned. If a psychologist, for example, has been doing assessments as a primary function for a school district, an increase or change in services should be preceded by some verbal or written announcements. The psy-chologist might visit faculty meetings and explain consultation, emphasize confidentiality, identify the goals or improvements anticipated, and gener-ally educate the consultee to use consultation services. Such an announce-ment should include elements of one-downsmanship. The consultant should show deference to the consultees' expertise and emphasize a desire to lighten the load on the consultees.

Because early consultation efforts might be misunderstood as attempts at offering psychotherapy, the consultant must use techniques to avoid the provision of psychotherapy. If this is not done, direct service to clients might be replaced by direct service to caregivers. Guidelines include the following:

1. Ask mainly objective, not personal, questions.
2. Discuss problems by discussing the client, not the consultee.
3. Do not let the consultee's anxiety over a case control consultant responses. Being empathic does not imply being unable to tolerate strong emotions surrounding problem solving.
4. Learn tactful but quick interruptions when a consultee is disclosing too much personal information. For example, "There's so much going on in your life at home! How is it affecting you at work?" Or, "You are sounding somewhat overwhelmed. Would it be helpful for me to recommend some good counselors to you?"

There are certain consultation postulates that must be gradually taught to consultees. When consultees come to see problems as consultants do, the chances for consultation becoming well established are improved. These postulates are as follows:

1. The setting is always part of the problem.
2. Effective problem-solving behaviors can be learned.
3. Help must be located near the setting.
4. The help offered must have the potential for being established on a systematic basis using the natural resources in the setting.
5. Errors are inevitable.
6. Efforts will be misunderstood.

The blending of direct and indirect service is often more of a reconceptualization on the part of the service provider (see Conoley & Gutkin, 1986a; Gutkin & Conoley, 1990) than a dramatic shift in the practitioner's activities. When psychologists realize that almost all their good ideas with children must be implemented by teachers or parents, the need to focus on adults and consider consultation as the primary service delivery system is obvious.

It is important to remember that most adults in school settings are doing what they feel they can do. It may seem a pittance from the consultant's perspective, but that is part of the consultation problem—to help people do more than they thought they could do. A consultant increases the chances that consultees will learn new skills by being cognizant of how to facilitate treatment suggestions.

ACCEPTABILITY OF
CONSULTATION
INTERVENTIONS

The implementation of an intervention designed by a consultee and consultant may be the most critical ingredient of consultation. Although other process outcomes are possible due to consultation, most consultants are concerned if teachers never implement the plans that have been jointly decided on.

What are the crucial variables to consider about implementation? Wolf (1978) proposed acceptability of treatments as an important construct for investigating the failure of follow-through. Kazdin (1980b) asserted that although a treatment may be effective, it may be viewed as inappropriate, unfair, unreasonable, or too intrusive.

Acceptability is an important construct because a consultant may be certain that if a consultee performed a recommended intervention the difficulty with the client (issue, organizational concern, etc.) would be resolved. But for some reason the consultee decides not to implement the intervention. Research into acceptability has been valuable for understanding which issues within a given social context affect whether a consultee uses an intervention. The consultant must understand how a treatment can be presented to make the interventions more acceptable and therefore more likely to be implemented.

CONCEPTUAL MODELS OF UNDERSTANDING ACCEPTABILITY

A reflection on several conceptual models of acceptability may provide an overview of this important topic. Witt and Elliott (1985) identified four elements that lead to a consultee using an intervention: acceptability, treatment use, integrity, and effectiveness. Furthering this model, Reimers, Wacker, and Koeppl (1987) suggested that acceptability depends on understanding, effectiveness, and minimal disruption of previous behavior patterns. If these requirements are met, the intervention is likely to be implemented and maintained.

A model that we find helpful incorporates elements of the Witt and Elliott (1985) and Reimers et al. (1987) models while broadening the categories. The model (see Figure 5.2) highlights the importance of the consultee's perceptions. How the consultee views the intervention is the critical feature contributing to whether the intervention is acceptable and, thus, is attempted.

The categories contributing to acceptability are the consultee's problem formulation, the consultee's beliefs about the intervention (integrity, effectiveness, understanding, amount of disruption), and the relationship (interaction) of the consultant with the consultee.

For the consultee to intervene, the intervention must be viewed as acceptable and the consultee must be able to perform the intervention.

Intervention Acceptability	=	Consultee's perception of fit between problem and intervention	+	Consultee's beliefs about the intervention level of difficulty, effectiveness, humaneness	+	Consultant-consultee relationship
Intervention Implementation	=	Intervention acceptability	+	Consultee's ability to implement intervention		
Intervention Maintenance	=	Intervention implementation	+	Tolerable disruption	+	Sufficient change created by the intervention

FIGURE 5.2. Model of intervention acceptability, implementation, and maintenance.

Performing the intervention may be as simple as the consultee having the skills and knowledge, or as complex as obtaining permission and/or cooperation from other school staff and parents. To maintain an intervention over a period of time, the consultee must perform the intervention, find the intervention within tolerable limits of disrupting typical classroom life, and believe that sufficient change is occurring. If these conditions are met, the consultant was successful in dealing with the consultee's identified problem. The following discussion focuses on achieving acceptability.

CONSULTEE'S PROBLEM FORMULATION

The consultee will have an understanding of the problem and will have developed feelings toward the child before the consultant arrives on the scene. It is likely that the consultee has been spending a great deal of time thinking about and interacting with the child. The immediate threat to treatment acceptability is whether the consultee and consultant judgments about the child match. Consultee perceptions that must be considered are seriousness, cause and purpose, problem description, and current affect toward the child.

Perceived Seriousness of a Problem

Consultees almost always have perceptions about the seriousness of a problem. The perceived severity of a problem is an interesting issue because if the problem is not viewed as severe, the consultee will not be willing to spend much time or effort intervening. A perception of increased severity predicts that the consultee will be more open to a variety of interventions and more willing to spend more time and effort on intervention (Witt, Martens, & Elliott, 1984). If the problem is viewed as too severe, however, the consultee may believe the solution is beyond his or her abilities and must become someone else's responsibility.

When there is a difference between the consultant and consultee regarding the perceived seriousness of a problem, the consultant should judge whether this difference will hamper a helpful problem formulation or treatment plan. For example, if the consultee is more concerned about a child's behavior than the consultant thinks is appropriate, what strategies are available to promote a shared treatment plan? The consultee may be expecting greater concern from the consultant or a more impressive intervention. When this discrepancy occurs, it is helpful to test the consultee's flexibility about viewing the problem less tragically. If the consultee does not reevaluate the severity, then a good strategy is to mirror the consultee's concern and break the problem into component parts; choose a component that both can agree is contributing to the problem and then design an intervention for the component. A typical rationale for this is that the whole problem cannot be resolved with one intervention, and choosing a goal that can be accomplished boosts the confidence of all concerned.

If the problem was of low severity, as the consultant suspected, then the intervention may solve the difficulty. The consultant can explain this success by noting that targeting a central issue for intervention clears up many other associated problems.

Perceived Cause and Purpose of a Problem

The cause and purpose of a child's behavior are similar issues. Depending on the consultee's working theory of human behavior (or of this problem in particular), the perceptions held concerning cause and/or purpose of the problem may be relatively important. If the consultee considers etiology and purpose to be critical aspects of the problem, then discrepancies between the consultant and consultee's beliefs are signals for potential problems in acceptability. For example, the purpose of a behavior can be seen sympathetically (e.g., crying for help, trying to be like other children, just having a little fun) or punitively (e.g., trying to hurt others, self-enhancing at the expense of others).

The consultee might perceive the cause of a behavior as most influential in deciding on acceptable treatment. For instance, if a consultee resists the idea of a limit-setting intervention because the child is apparently the victim of a poor home environment, what can the consultant say to increase the probability of intervention implementation? Understanding the importance of causal attributions, the consultant would be well advised to construct an explanation of the treatment that underscores that caring adults set limits for children and children cannot be expected to understand this difficult but critical adult responsibility (Conoley, Conoley, Ivey, & Scheel, in press).

Problem Description

An issue that is basic to the acceptability of an intervention is matching the intervention to the problem description. If the intervention seems unrelated to the problem, the consultee will find it less acceptable. A consultant may have a different way of seeing a problematic situation, but a consultee wants a suggestion that fits what he or she has found intolerable. It is important to use the consultee's language about the problem when describing the intervention. The consultee should perceive that the consultant's suggestions are meeting his or her needs. Sometimes consultants resist working on the problem as defined by the consultee. As Haley (1977) pointed out, this resistance on the part of the consultant leads to high attrition rates and, therefore, reduces the chances that the consultee will attempt any intervention.

If consultees use global problem descriptions such as poor self-esteem, the consultant must investigate what child behaviors are responsible for that diagnosis and link suggestions to those behaviors. If consultees do not see the connection between intervention and problem, they are more likely to discontinue or never begin a treatment.

Feelings Toward the Child

The consultee will almost always have some affective response to the identified problem. Teachers and parents report a desire to to avoid using reductive interventions or interventions that are viewed as punitive (Elliott, Witt, Galvin, & Peterson, 1984; Kazdin, 1980a, 1980b, 1981; Martens, Peterson, Witt, & Cirone, 1986; Witt, Elliott, & Martens, 1984; Witt & Robins, 1985).

Although these studies may represent parent and teacher responses in analogue situations reacting to written descriptions of a child's problem, our experience indicates that teachers and parents in direct contact with real children who are irritating and noncompliant are, in fact, often blaming, harsh, and punitive as well as more motivated to intervene. The existence of negative emotion tends to inhibit the consultee's implementation of any intervention construed as kindly toward the child. Consultees often erroneously believe that any encouragement or reinforcement of a troubling child will be construed as giving in to the child, or they report that they cannot be positive when they feel angry.

Consultants must be skilled at identifying incompatible behaviors for the consultee to reward and providing the needed rationale for attention to acceleration targets (i.e., appropriate behaviors that we wish increased). Further, if a consultee is "burned out" by a child, plans that require a large amount of consultee input are probably impractical. A consultant might consider using another adult as the primary intervenor, teaching the child self-monitoring skills, suggesting some group contingencies so the class is responsible for the reinforcement, and so on.

BELIEFS ABOUT AN INTERVENTION

The consultee must view the intervention with enough optimism that at least initial attempts at implementation are made. Beliefs about an intervention include (a) whether the intervention fits the consultee's theoretical beliefs, (b) whether the intervention is viewed as effective, and (c) whether the intervention is viewed as worth the time and effort.

Theoretical Fit

Many teachers identify themselves as most influenced by some well-known theory of human behavior. Even if the exact name of the theoretical school eludes them, a consultant who listens carefully will often uncover how consultees make sense of others' behavior. The consultant can then use similar wording and reasoning to match the consultee's (Conoley, Conoley, Ivey, & Scheel, in press).

Any effective intervention can be described using humanistic, pragmatic, behavioral, or other terms (Kazdin & Cole, 1981; Witt, Martens, & Elliott, 1984; Woolfolk & Woolfolk, 1979). Therefore, when the consultant discusses an intervention, the description can match the theoretical beliefs of the consultee, thus increasing the acceptability of the intervention.

Effectiveness

A consultee may have used many interventions prior to the current situation and developed opinions about many more by talking with others. The personal experience of the consultee regarding an intervention's success influences acceptability. Disputing a consultee's personal experience is probably a waste of time. A consultant should be creative enough to think of alternative strategies even if the consultee's opinion is based on an incomplete understanding or a misapplication of an intervention.

If the intervention in question is the only alternative, then the consultant must learn exactly how it was implemented previously or on what the consultee's concerns are based. It may be possible to give an old intervention a new look by making minor changes. The consultant can validate the consultee's concerns by agreeing that the old understanding of an intervention was problematic for many people, but new modifications have been shown to be improvements.

Time and Effort

The consultee will have to consider the amount of time and effort that is available to implement the intervention. Time demand is an important acceptability dimension (Elliott et al., 1984; Kazdin, 1982; Witt & Martens, 1983; Witt, Elliott, & Martens, 1984; Witt, Martens, & Elliott, 1984). Consultees may see a 30-minute daily intervention as reasonable but an hour-long daily intervention as impossible. Witt, Martens, and Elliott (1984) found that consultees are willing to spend more time intervening for problems they perceive as severe.

In describing an intervention plan, consultants may be tempted to underestimate the time needed for implementation. It may not be advisable, however, to underestimate the time but rather to underscore how an investment now will prevent more troubling problems.

Labeling the problem as severe may encourage the consultee to invest in intervention. For example, a teacher may be willing to spend more time to help a depressed child than a noncompliant child. Because it is often true that depressed children are noncompliant, this interpretation of the behavior may predict more successful treatment implementation.

Relationship Between Consultee and Consultant

If the consultee sees the consultant as credible, acceptability increases. A consultant with a proven track record or positive reputation with the consultee is likely to suggest ideas that consultees find more acceptable. The dimensions of expertness and trustworthiness as perceived by the consultee enhance consultant effectiveness.

ACCEPTABILITY SUMMARY

An intervention that consultees perceive as acceptable will likely be implemented. To assess if a sufficient level of acceptability has been reached, the consultant should listen from the beginning of consultation sessions for the issues mentioned in the preceding sections. Consultants should also listen for differences between their view and the way the consultee describes and understands the problems. They should notice the emotional stance of the consultee. Difficulties may surface if the consultee is too sympathetic or too angry about the situation. When it is time to suggest an intervention, there are several important issues. The consultant should use vocabulary that matches the consultee's theory or manner of speaking about the problem; be certain to link the desired outcome of the intervention to the identified problem; and use rationales for the intervention that match the consultee's way of understanding the problem and feelings about the situation.

Consultants often feel ready to recommend an intervention soon after witnessing or hearing about a problem. The issue of intervention acceptability underscores the importance of knowing more about the consultee's perspective before plunging ahead with treatment recommendations. Any strategy's acceptability can be enhanced if the rationale used to describe it is consistent with the consultee's needs and current conceptualizations (Conoley, Conoley, Ivey, & Scheel, in press).

PREREFERRAL TEAMS

Prereferral, student assistance, or intervention assistance teams are potential levers for implementing a consultation program (Chalfant, Pysh, & Moultrice, 1979; Curtis, Curtis, & Graden, 1988; Graden, Casey, & Christenson, 1985). Now mandated in several states, the teams are composed of specially trained teachers who serve as consultants to their colleagues. Depending on the situation, other experts might be invited to problem-solve with the team. The goals are to deal with students in the classroom (perhaps avoiding expensive special education services) and increase teacher repertoires in handling behavioral and instructional challenges. The opportunities for consultants are obvious.

These teams provide a group consultation model that might be expanded in many helpful ways. For example, in addition to dealing with particular student problems, teams might tackle faculty morale issues, plan faculty development experiences, or study system-wide difficulties associated with at-risk children. Implementing and supporting such teams can provide consultants with access to teachers at many grade levels.

School-based problem solving has positive outcomes for students, teachers, parents, and administrators. A staff that pools its resources and talents to meet learning, behavioral, and emotional needs of children is likely to (a) create innovative solutions to difficult problems; (b) address concerns early, thereby increasing probabilities of success; (c) develop through the sharing of professional expertise; (d) sustain a positive, coping school environment; and (e) be open to input from parents, specialists, and administrators regarding strategies for managing learning environments.

The prerequisites for attaining these positive outcomes include availability of problem-solving teams in the school; substantial support from administrators for implementing a problem-solving sequence; specialized training of staff in problem solving; and an openness among the staff to identify problems, help others with concerns, and recognize that student problems are the products of student, peer group, teacher, parent, and task characteristics. This final component may be most critical. Problem solving based only on student characteristics is likely to be incomplete.

Logistics of a Team

The teams often operate along the following lines:

1.   The teacher recognizes a problem in meeting the learning needs of a child.

2.   After unsuccessful classroom interventions, the teacher contacts the chairperson of the prereferral team.

3.   These two staff members confer to determine a useful problem definition and identify resource personnel to assist the teacher.

4.   The chairperson arranges a problem-solving meeting with the staff chosen by the teacher or with the prereferral team in the building, facilitates that meeting, provides follow-up support, and may reconvene that group or another at the request of the teacher or in response to the plan devised by the group.

5.   The teacher and chairperson are free to choose as problem-solving resources any school-based, district-based, community-based resource. These may include (but are not limited to) educational specialists, other classroom teachers, special education teachers, school psychologists, building administrators, school counselors, parents, physicians, and community agency personnel. Many schools have an established team that is always used for some specified period of time.

6.   The prereferral team chairperson keeps records of the outcomes associated with the process and makes these available to school principals and staff to evaluate and improve the process in subsequent years.

Advantages and Disadvantages of Prereferral Teams

Advantages. Implementation of school-based problem solving is effective because it is close to the source of the difficulty. Involving a wide array of specialists and other experts to support the teacher brings needed expertise and emphasizes that troubled children are the entire community's concern. Perhaps more important is the development of a cadre of teachers who act as consultants to each other. This process requires training, but it can be the source of positive organizational change—for example, change away from the perception of teaching as a lonely profession to one of teaching as a collaborative enterprise.

Disadvantages. The involvement of many individuals suggests a training problem. How will everyone who may be asked to serve on a team be trained in problem solving? Further, how will teachers and other specialists be recognized for this work? Will they be given enough time to assist others while still performing their own duties?

These are real problems that can be solved. To do so, however, requires commitment and resources. Time must be set aside for training, team meetings, team activities (oberservation, modeling, etc.), and coordination with other specialists. Money will have to be made available to support training efforts and release time for team members.

The intervention assistance process has been introduced to schools with astounding success in the overall functioning of the school. There have been situations, however, in which the team was a mere response to the external mandate to have a team. No real problem solving was attempted, and teachers who approached the teams saw them as obstacles to getting their children needed special education services. Principal support made the difference between successful and unsuccessful teams.

Implementing Intervention Assistance Teams

The following steps are important for implementing prereferral teams.

1.   School personnel are informed about the nature and purposes of the teams and given meaningful input into preparation and design.

2.   Some process is determined by which the chairperson of the team is chosen.

3.   The chairperson should receive substantial support to learn problem solving, consultation, and resource identification. For example, this person will have to assist the teacher in problem identification, facilitate the group meeting, be aware of school and community resources, and follow up with each teacher and monitor the outcomes associated with the entire process.

4.   The entire staff should receive some in-service training on problem solving and consultation. This can provide a basis of understanding so teachers approach the prereferral teams for assistance.

5.   Written documentation of the process, guidelines, directory of resources, and so on might be produced as part of preparing for the teams.

Evaluation

The following are suggestions for evaluating the prereferral teams:

1. *Usage:* How many teachers (or other staff) use the plan?
2. *Staff perceptions:* Of those who use the process, what are their reactions? Of those who do not choose to use it, what are their reasons? What are the reactions of those chosen to serve on the teams? What are the perceptions of the chairperson? Is the role of the chairperson seen as a prestigious position? What is the school principal's perception? Is staff more problem oriented; is staff being utilized more fully; is the school climate improved?
3. *Outcomes:* What are the outcomes of the process in terms of goals being met? This might involve classroom observation, teacher report, parent report, student perceptions, and so on.
4. *Renewal:* Is staff input being utilized to fine-tune the approach? Who is in charge of making changes, monitoring the continuing implementation, and evaluating the approach?

The foregoing issues are similar to evaluation targets discussed in chapter 7. Notice that the questions consider the effects of prereferral teams on the individual and organizational level. Evaluation of the teams should investigate all operational levels in the school.

INSTRUCTIONAL
CONSULTATION

A consultant can maximize the fit between the school organization and his or her service delivery system by being an expert in instruction. Instructional consultation is described fully by Rosenfield (1987). Measurement issues associated with instructional consultation are explored by Lentz and Shapiro (1986).

The instructional consultant must develop an organizational framework with which to view the classroom activities of teachers and students and an expertise in examining the tasks children are given to accomplish. Helpful resources exist (e.g., Larivee, 1985; Reynolds, 1979, 1989).

Reynolds (1979, 1989) has identified ten major competency areas necessary for successful teaching and mainstreaming. He asserts that teachers must have expertise in: (a) curriculum development; (b) teaching basic skills; (c) classroom management; (d) professional consultation and communication; (e) teacher-parent-student relationships; (f) student-student relationships; (g) an understanding of exceptional conditions and special needs; (h) a working understanding of the referral process; (i) professional values; and (j) individualized teaching.

Effective Instruction

A related framework has been proposed by Ysseldyke and Christenson (1986). They have organized twelve critical components of effective instruction and developed a scale to assess the nature of children's instructional environment. Even if one does not use the scale, the components provide a comprehensive description of positive classroom ecology and thus the basis of instructional consultation. The following information is adapted from the Ysseldyke and Christenson scale manual (pp. 42–55). A similar list of critical components of effective instruction derived from research efforts can be found in Larrivee (1985).

Instructional Presentation. This component of effective instruction includes factors related to lesson development, clarity of directions, and checking for student understanding. Some behaviors that indicate effectiveness on this component are: (a) concrete examples are used in the instructional lesson; (b) the student's attention is gained before task directions are given; and (c) initial problems are checked within the first 10 minutes of independent seatwork activities.

Classroom Environment. An effective classroom environment is created by skills in classroom management, productive use of time, and the affective tone or class climate. Some descriptors of each of these elements are: (a) nonverbal signals are used to redirect a student while the teacher is teaching other students; (b) transitions are short; and (c) the classroom is characterized by a cooperative rather than competitive atmosphere.

Teacher Expectations. Teachers should have high, yet realistic expectations for student performance, including task completion, quality of work, and the use of time in the classroom. For example, a student should clearly know what the consequences of achieving or not achieving certain expected standards of performance are.

Cognitive Emphasis. In addition to teaching content, effective classrooms emphasize thinking skills. For example, a teacher can model how to think through the steps involved in solving a problem. In addition, the purposes of different lessons in terms of thinking skills should be clearly identified (e.g., memorizing, reasoning, concluding, or evaluating).

Motivational Strategies. Effective teachers understand various methods for increasing children's interest in lessons. Some of these are enthusiasm in presentation, use of novel ways of presenting information, and careful monitoring of students' success rates.

Relevant Practice. Students spend significant time practicing what they have learned, often during independent seatwork assignments. This time is used most wisely if teachers are skilled in: (a) practice opportunity; (b) task relevance; and (c) instructional material. These skills are evident in classrooms where students are given sufficient opportunity for the practice of skills and content, where students have acquired the necessary prerequisite skills to complete the task successfully, and necessary modification for successful completion of assignments are made (e.g., length varied, content simplified, concrete aids and cues provided).

Academic Engaged Time. Both the opportunity to engage in academic work and the speed with which work is completed influence achievement levels. Teachers must be effective in keeping students involved and maintaining student engagement. Some indications that students are involved are that students spend little time sitting and waiting and that alternative academic options are available to students who have completed their assignments.

Informed Feedback. The provision of specific, informative feedback and corrective procedures are necessary steps in successfully instructing students. Feedback is provided by giving task-specific praise about the student's academic work. Corrective procedures include giving the student an immediate chance to correctly practice a procedure or execute a task after an error has been identified.

Adaptive Instruction. Instruction must be modified to accommodate individual needs and differences. Adaptive instruction refers to a systematic effort to adjust curriculum to increase students' success. An example of this activity is a teacher's willingness to use different materials, alternative teaching strategies, increased practice opportunities, or alternative group placement to assist a student who fails to master an objective.

Progress Evaluation. Effective instruction includes continuous monitoring and systematic follow-up planning for a student. Examples of each include: (a) homework is checked, graded and reviewed with the student; and (b) review and maintenance activities are planned systematically (daily, weekly, monthly).

Instructional Planning. Instructional planning includes two functions: diagnosis and prescription. Examples of each are that the gap between the student's actual and desired levels of performance is stated clearly, and that the instructional process is guided by the objective or goal to be achieved rather than workbook pages to be completed.

Student Understanding. Student understanding refers to the accuracy with which the student understands the instructional goal and interprets the task directions and the processes necessary to complete a task. Evidence that student understanding is appropriate can be inferred from the student's success rate during independent practice activities. Appropriate rates are between 90% and 100%. Even students who appear to be working can misunderstand a lesson. One student, apparently low on student understanding, answered a query, "What are you doing?" with "I don't know, but I'm done."

Conclusion

The empirical basis for excellent instruction provides a useful springboard for school consultation. A consultant who is an expert in instructional consultation is likely to be credible to educators. A child's success with academic work is a significant accomplishment and deserves energetic support from consultants.

NO FINAL SOLUTIONS

No service delivery system is optimal in every organization all of the time. The services must be responsive to developmental changes and flexible enough to use the diverse talents of many service providers. The consultant is necessarily always in a dynamic state of tension concerning how best to assist a particular organization because the organization is always in a dynamic state of tension maintained by internal changes, external demands, and interface exchanges.

There is a tendency to create structures in response to organizational needs and then see these structures as eternally correct. The developers feel unwilling to undo something that has worked in the past even when its usefulness has declined.

Living systems always change, but the changes may be imperceptible. Sensitivity to these changes and ability to assess and compare organizational needs over time are crucial aspects of successful service delivery. The emphasis on direct and indirect services may shift in response to system shifts. A sudden influx of new clients (e.g., children of illegal aliens heretofore denied public education) may move a psychological service delivery system toward increased direct services to children and families. That move must be remembered as a response to a historical event, not as a new policy.

In planning for change in service delivery, planners must balance vision with context. Neither the vision nor the context is more or less real. Awareness of both is necessary. Without a vision of how the world should be, planners have no way to develop strategies. Without a knowledge of their particular moment in history, they have no chance to see their dreams realized.

SUMMARY

Despite the generally supportive research associated with consultation effectiveness across a large number of presenting problems, implementation barriers persist. Some of the barriers arise because of consultants who may lack training or conviction about the efficacy of a particular form of service delivery. Other barriers arise because of consultees who are not prepared to use consultation or administrators who are either suspicious of the consultant or protective against intrusions into their staffs' planning times.

Moving beyond the barriers requires a host of skills in planning, patience, and sensitivity. An awareness of the research regarding the acceptability of interventions provides a framework for suggesting consultation plans that teachers may find useful and effective. In addition, the development of intervention assistance teams is an important springboard to consultation service.

SUGGESTED READINGS

Fish, M. C., & Jain, S. (1988). Using systems theory in school assessment and intervention: A structural model for school psychologists. *Professional School Psychology, 3,* 291–300.

Graden, J. L., Zins, J. E., & Curtis, M. J. (1988). *Alternative educational delivery systems: Enhancing instructional options for all students.* Washington, DC: National Association of School Psychologists.

Gutkin, T. B., & Conoley, J. C. (1990). Reconceptualizing school psychology from a service delivery perspective: Implications for practice, training, and research. *Journal of School Psychology, 28,* 203–223.

Medway, F. J., & Updyke, J. F. (1985). Meta-analysis of consultation outcome studies. *American Journal of Community Psychology, 13,* 489–504.

Meyers, J., Pfeffer, J., & Erlbaum, V. (1985). Process assessment: A model for broadening assessment. *Journal of Special Education, 19,* 73–89.

Plas, J. M. (1986). *Systems psychology in the schools.* Elmsford, NY: Pergamon Press.

Chapter 6

Evaluation Issues and Strategies in Consultation

A number of authors have summarized and analyzed the state of research on consultation efficacy (see Gresham & Kendell, 1987; Mannino & Shore, 1979; Medway, 1979; Pryzwansky, 1986). These reviews are of particular interest to researchers and trainers. Typical consultation research may provide helpful ideas for practice, but much of the research has little relevance to consultants' daily work. Few working consultants without university affiliation can spare the time to manipulate one variable in the consultation experience to study its effect on outcomes (e.g., Conoley & Conoley, 1982).

All consultants are, however, interested in making judgments about the value of their services to a particular host organization (e.g., Fairchild, 1976; Gutkin, Henning-Stout, & Piersel, 1988). This distinction between truth and value lies at the heart of the difference between research and evaluation (Matuszek, 1981). It will make little difference to a consultee organization if the consultant does everything with textbook perfection. The decision makers are interested in positive outcomes in terms of cost, increased services, or staff feedback. Consultants must be prepared not only to provide assistance to others who are planning, implementing, and evaluating programs (i.e., program consultation) but must also give priority to such activities in their own service delivery systems.

To accomplish a good evaluation, consultants must know at least the following:

• What their goals are;
• What the goals of the organization are;
• Which consultation techniques appear preferable;

• Which evaluation methods are feasible; and,
• What outcomes are expected.

These general points also comprise the consultation contract (see chapter 5). A well-done contract can provide the basis for the evaluation plan.

Evaluation is not relegated to the final moment of a consultation venture. In fact, if consultants wait until the last few weeks of a consultation program to begin data collection, they have missed the point of both consultation and evaluation. Good consultants seek ongoing feedback. Good evaluators plan on collecting data throughout a program so they can answer various formative evaluation questions like the following:

1. Are consultees aware of the consultation service?
2. Do consultees understand the parameters of consultation?
3. How many requests for consultation are made during specified time periods?
4. How much consultation is going on during specified time periods?
5. What are the typical problems addressed in consultation?
6. How successful are various cases according to consultee feedback and client outcome?
7. Is the consultant spending the agreed-on time with the organization?
8. Is consultation actually taking place, or are other activities more prevalent?
9. Are timelines attached to meeting certain goals?
10. With increasing knowledge about the system, does consultation still appear the most preferable strategy?

Even this abbreviated list may seem overwhelming at first. Consultants may wonder when they provide service if they spend so much time in data collection. Two considerations are relevant. First, the ability to gather such data depends on planning before the consultation begins. Experience will suggest different strategies. Second, it is shortsighted to believe that quality services can be provided in an information vacuum.

What is gained by answering the aforementioned questions? What is lost by not knowing the answers? Our experience indicates that quality services and invitations to return to do more consultation result from knowing the answers.

PROCESS AND PRODUCT EVALUATIONS

Many writers in evaluation theory and practice point out the complementary aspects of process (formative) and product (summative) evaluations (e.g., Borich, 1974; Hayman & Napier, 1975). Generally, process evaluation refers to data collection that monitors whether the program is going as planned. For example, has the consultant been working 4 hours every day? In addition, process evaluation keeps abreast of interim time-lines or instrumental goals. For example, has the consultant met all the important organization administrators within the first 3 weeks of work? Product evaluation is aimed at determining the final outcomes of the program (i.e., were objectives met?). For example, did consultation services result in a decrease in direct service referrals?

The two types of evaluation are not separate entities because a hierar-chical or sequential structure is implicit. If the program was never imple-mented as planned, the chances for outcome success appear slight.

Despite the interdependence of evaluation types, most evaluations are conceived narrowly or solely as product evaluations; that is, practitioners wait until the end of a program and examine whether objectives were achieved. Sole reliance on product evaluation is problematic for the fol-lowing reasons:

1.   Self-correcting feedback is a necessary component of every service delivery system. Process evaluation provides the opportunity for ongoing program modifications.

2.   All program planning requires hypothetical elements. Some conse-quences of action can be anticipated but unintended outcomes are inevita-ble (Sarason, 1982). Process evaluation can provide data for analysis and interpretation throughout the implementation phase of a program, and thus monitor both deleterious and serendipitous effects of unintended consequences.

SAMPLE EVALUATION STRATEGIES

A number of process data collection strategies can be employed. If consultants are employees of an organization, they probably already re-spond to certain data-gathering mandates. Much of these data, although potentially helpful, are either too late or looked at only as product or accountability data. Consultants may have to keep concurrent records to meet their own evaluation needs. They also might target the efficient use of collected data as a consultative goal.

Logs of activities are helpful. These might be relatively structured checklists or accounts of subjective impressions. An advantage of check-lists is standardized information across all cases and relatively effortless accomplishment. A disadvantage is that no checklist accounts for all that may happen; therefore, important impressions, events, or facts may not be recorded because there are no appropriate categories.

Relatively unstructured logs are easy to put off doing and may result in gaps in detail across some cases. On the other hand, writing gut reactions, plans for the future, and vague impressions is a rewarding activity that everyone should try at least temporarily.

Special checklists can be constructed to match particular objectives. For example, consultants might list all of their potential consultees and then check and date the names as each is met and some preliminary entry is accomplished. Other data regarding problems, efficacy, methodologies, and data gathering can be consolidated in logs as well.

The progress notes illustrated in chapter 2 (Figure 2.1) are also helpful process devices. These can serve the dual functions of facilitating the problem-solving process and providing data relating to quantity and quality of services.

Ecological Evaluation

Evaluation strategies should be sensitive to the targets and operational levels that consultants choose. A plan to evaluate a consultation program for an organization or individual consultees should be reviewed using ecological criteria to ensure comprehensiveness.

Microsystems. The consultant must seek feedback concerning efficacy and self-monitor his or her skills (i.e., conduct microsystem evaluation; see Table 6.1) and must further seek information about outcomes at each operational level and about each consultation target. Typical sources of data are consultees, supervisors, and clients.

Positive evaluations from consultees are crucial but probably insufficient as a comprehensive evaluation plan. Whenever possible, data should be collected from consultees concerning their use of consultation, their impressions of the consultant, and the perceived effects of consultation on the targeted case. In addition, the consultant should do some direct observation or measurement of client changes. These measurements may take the form of classroom observation and clients' academic records, or staff meeting observation and employee productivity records when the consultee organization is a business.

A special note on measurement may be in order. There are numerous occasions in a consultation program when the consultee seeks support from the consultant. The consultee does not expect problem resolution — just a sympathetic ear and some words of encouragement. These instances are not trivial and should be part of an evaluative program. Evaluation questions should include open-ended comments from consultees, which may allow some of these positive or negative feelings to surface for interpretation and action (see Table 6.2).

Table 6.1. Consultant Trainee Evaluation Form

Date of evaluation:
Consultant:
Supervisor:
Directions: The ratings of consultants should be based on actual observation and/or reports received from staff, parents, students, and so on regarding consultant performance. Circle the number of the scale that best describes the consultant's competence as given in the description below. Rate each category independently. A description of scale points is provided below.

1—competence considered to be in need of further training and/or require additional growth, maturation, and change on the part of the consultant for him or her to be effective in the various skill areas;

2—competence currently considered to be below average but with further supervision and experience is expected to develop satisfactorily; close supervision is required;

3—competence at least at minimal level necessary for functioning with moderate supervision required;

4—competence assessed to be above average, suggesting a minimal need for supervision;

5—competencies developed and reflect capability for independent functioning with little or no supervision required;

No data—insufficient data to make rating at this time.

General competencies	Rating					
1. *Evaluation—assessment*						
Intellectual	1	2	3	4	5	No data
Social and emotional	1	2	3	4	5	No data
Interviewing skills	1	2	3	4	5	No data
Behavioral assessment	1	2	3	4	5	No data
Personality assessment	1	2	3	4	5	No data
Curriculum-based assessment	1	2	3	4	5	No data
Environmental assessment	1	2	3	4	5	No data
Neuropsychological assessment	1	2	3	4	5	No data
Family assessment	1	2	3	4	5	No data
Ability to integrate data	1	2	3	4	5	No data
Other _____	1	2	3	4	5	No data
2. *Intervention*						
Practicality	1	2	3	4	5	No data
Appropriateness to problems	1	2	3	4	5	No data
Specificity of recommendations	1	2	3	4	5	No data
Conceptual clarity	1	2	3	4	5	No data
Provision for follow-up	1	2	3	4	5	No data
Implementation	1	2	3	4	5	No data
Actual follow-up	1	2	3	4	5	No data
Flexibility	1	2	3	4	5	No data
3. *Communication and collaboration*						
Staff conferencing	1	2	3	4	5	No data
Parent conferencing	1	2	3	4	5	No data
Administrative conferencing	1	2	3	4	5	No data
Case staffing	1	2	3	4	5	No data
Report writing	1	2	3	4	5	No data
Use of supervisory input	1	2	3	4	5	No data
4. *Consultation*						
Problem and need identification	1	2	3	4	5	No data
Plan formulation	1	2	3	4	5	No data
Plan implementation	1	2	3	4	5	No data
Follow-up and evaluation	1	2	3	4	5	No data

(Continued)

Table 6.1. *(Continued)*

	Family consultation	1	2	3	4	5	No data
	Primary caregiver consultation	1	2	3	4	5	No data
5.	*Teaching and workshop skills*						
	Planning	1	2	3	4	5	No data
	Implementation	1	2	3	4	5	No data
	Evaluation	1	2	3	4	5	No data
6.	*Interpersonal style*						
	Confidentiality	1	2	3	4	5	No data
	Enthusiasm	1	2	3	4	5	No data
	Dependability	1	2	3	4	5	No data
	Promptness	1	2	3	4	5	No data
	Creativity	1	2	3	4	5	No data
	Productivity	1	2	3	4	5	No data
	Rapport with						
	clients	1	2	3	4	5	No data
	staff	1	2	3	4	5	No data
	parents	1	2	3	4	5	No data
7.	*Research and program evaluation*						
	Planning	1	2	3	4	5	No data
	Implementation	1	2	3	4	5	No data
	Provision for subject rights	1	2	3	4	5	No data
	Provision for confidentiality	1	2	3	4	5	No data
8.	*Overall rating of the consultant*	1	2	3	4	5	No data

Please summarize any consultant strengths or weaknesses not mentioned on the above rating scale. Note any training experiences that should be planned for this consultant.

Supervisors' reactions to consultation are also important to monitor. Such monitoring may take the form of face-to-face meetings during which the consultant asks for feedback, checks if the supervisor has questions, asks if the supervisor has had feedback from other staff members, brings the supervisor up to date on consultation activities, and probes to see if the standing contract is still satisfactory. It is good to establish a norm for open communication of this sort.

Consultants must stay aware of the time constraints of supervisors, however, and not appear too demanding of supervisor time. Some supervisors prefer written communications either preceding or following face-to-face meetings. Although keeping written records of ongoing cases is a difficult process, such records can become invaluable for final reporting to the consultee organization. Consultants can save copies of these as summaries of interactions with supervisors and as reminders of what occurred during consultation and what the consultant's and supervisor's interpretations were.

Mesosystem. Consultation often results in better case management and coordination of services for a client; that is, facilitating the cooperation of all the affected systems. Case management may be as simple as having teachers from two classrooms communicate about a child, or it may be a com-

Table 6.2. Open-Ended Consultation Evaluation Form

1. Compared with other teachers at your school, your contacts with the consultant were
   considerably fewer   fewer   average   more   considerably more

2. With what aspect of the consultation have you been happiest? Least happy? _____

3. What would you like to see changed? _____

4. How might the consultant be more available to you? _____

5. What comments or suggestions do you have about the consultant's work? _____

6. Based on what the consultant did, how would you define the role of the consultant?

7. Based on your experience with consultation this year, consultation is

extremely helpful						not at all helpful
7	6	5	4	3	2	1

plex process of integrating recommendations and demands from families, schools, judicial and legal, and social service agencies.

Process evaluation at a mesosystem level often takes the form of documenting that the right people have met to coordinate their efforts concerning a particular child or issue. Another possibility is ascertaining if information for improved collaboration has been shared with members of different systems. For example, the common pitfalls of coordinating behavioral plans between home and school are well known to most school-based consultants. Consultants should monitor whether they have prepared these two interdependent systems for cooperation by ensuring:

1. All parties understand exactly the changes expected of them.
    Everyone, teacher, parent, child, and so on, must agree to a change.
2. A feasible communication system between parents and teachers must be established.
3. The consultant must facilitate consistent follow-through on the parts of teachers and parents in terms of their behavior and the provision of rewards to children.

Cooperation is often aimed at discrete child behaviors but can be the vehicle for classroom and family change if all parties live up to their contracts. For example, parents who follow through with positive attention to a child who performs well at school are likely to improve not only the child's school work but also the parent-child relationship. Analogously, a teacher who communicates frequently with parents is likely to both be more successful with individual children and feel more supported by parents in doing difficult work.

A consultant interested in mesosystem evaluation should consider whether hoped-for changes due to coordination actually occur. Interviews, questionnaires, and observations are all possible evaluation methodologies.

Macrosystem. Macrosystem or societal change may be easy to evaluate (e.g., Has a law prohibiting corporal punishment of minor children been passed by a legislature?). Or it may be difficult to evaluate (e.g., Does the passage of the law have any effect on child abuse rates?). An individual consultant might gain access to important information by an affiliation with established advocacy agencies such as the Children's Defense Fund, Center on Human Policy, Association for Retarded Citizens, or Common Cause. The consultant's particular professional interests would suggest which groups might be most useful.

Consultants can be members of groups at local and regional levels that monitor important social changes. These could be professional groups, boards of social service agencies, or trustees of certain charitable organizations. Each group has some special interests that narrow the kind of data collected and may slant interpretations of data. Such effects are, however, unavoidable in a pluralistic society.

If consultants have been part of efforts to make some important social change, they should devote professional energy to evaluating their role and contributions. For example, a consultant who assists a parent group that is advocating for more effective special education placements can gather data on the known effectiveness (e.g., academic and behavioral improvements) of current practices, the goals the parents espouse, the discrepancy between the two (i.e., between the current and desired situations), and can assist in suggesting strategies for reaching the desired goals. A school-based consultant can assist in generating solutions that match the existing capabilities of schools so success in implementation is enhanced.

Consultants involved in such efforts need feedback from their constituent groups and from peer professionals. When working for social or organizational change, emotions often overtake reason. The consultant may find the generation of valid data difficult. Constituents may be favorably impressed with consultants when goals are reached but unfavorably impressed if goals elude the group. Although such outcome data are important, excellent efforts may have been expended in both situations.

EVALUATING CONSULTATION TRAINING

Not all practitioners have received training in consultation. It may be useful to consider the objectives of consultation courses nationwide to facilitate self-evaluation regarding needs for continuing education.

A review of many texts in the field and inspections of several consultation course syllabi suggest that well-known educators' learning objectives in consultation include the following:

1. Increase skills in conceptualizing school (and other) cultures and processes of change likely to match the cultural regularities.
2. Develop a repertoire of interventions with consultees to increase their effectiveness with clients and each other.
3. Develop skills in evaluation of service delivery programs.
4. Develop knowledge of consultation models.
5. Develop the ability to use theory to guide case conceptualization and intervention according to the presenting situation.
6. Develop the ability to synthesize a personal model of consultation intervention.
7. Develop skills in formulating problems in ways that facilitate resolution.
8. Develop expertise in listening and feedback skills.
9. Develop the ability to enter into and terminate smoothly individual consultative relationships.
10. Develop the ability to design and deliver in-service training to consultees.
11. Develop expertise in design and implementation of preventive mental health strategies.
12. Develop the ability to diagnose organizational variables and design, implement, and evaluate appropriate interventions.
13. Develop awareness of personal impact in the consultative relationship, including important ethical dimensions.
14. Apply a wide variety of assessment and intervention skills, especially behavioral analyses and interventions.

Readers can examine these objectives and decide whether they have mastered each of the targets. If not, workshops or graduate courses may be helpful for professional development.

Consultation education is different from other graduate training experiences. The professor or workshop leader is always modeling aspects of his or her consultation skills. This increases opportunities for students to learn consultation but compels the trainer to practice what is preached. Trainers are both evaluators as well as consultants and can maximize student learning by adopting as many consultation strategies as possible when teaching.

The typical evaluation procedures used in graduate classes and workshops are appropriate for consultation training such as assessments of information retention (e.g., tests, class discussions); organizational abilities (e.g., papers, reports); consulting skills (e.g., in-class role-plays, feedback from consultees or other supervisors); and interpersonal skills (e.g., mutual feedback sessions, teaming abilities, simulations). It may be good consultation training policy to allow students to resubmit written work until the criterion grade (at least a B) is earned. This allows for constructive supervisor input and thus provides additional modeling examples for the trainee.

In addition, consultation instructors should model openness to feedback and evaluation by regularly seeking input from their students. Regularly scheduled feedback sessions between instructors and students are important for the continued personal and professional growth of both.

Short- and long-term evaluations of education and training are desirable. Consultant trainees face predictable problems including the following:

1. How to enter an organization;
2. Never knowing enough about the problem or the organization;
3. Unpleasant relationships with consultees;
4. Role clarity as consultant;
5. Confidence in the efficacy of consultation; and
6. Meeting the direct service demands.

These difficulties have provided a framework for a helpful evaluation instrument, shown in Table 6.3.

RESEARCH AND SERVICE DILEMMAS

Consultation research and evaluation carried out in the applied settings creates research-related ethical issues. Informed consent, withholding of treatment of control groups, and maintenance of obviously failing treatments are a few examples of common dilemmas. Each of these can be resolved with careful planning.

In addition, more flexible, action-oriented research paradigms making use of process (formative) evaluation data must be conceptualized. Consultation is supposed to depend on the circumstances presented. Planning strict, inflexible consultation models meant to enhance experimental rigor underestimates the power of the models and badly serves the host organization. Experimental rigor aimed at increasing internal validity is necessarily accompanied by the loss of external validity.

The relative amounts of energy and creativity devoted to well-done research and service delivery must be carefully monitored throughout a research project. Consultees should be aware of the major focus if one activity is, in fact, more highly valued than the other. With such information, potential consultees can make better informed decisions regarding the consultation service.

Table 6.3. Evaluation of Consultant Field Competence in Consultation

A. *Entry into the school building or system.* How do you rate your skills at fitting in smoothly, reducing time between becoming familiar with the school and conducting actual professional activity?

1	2	3	4	5
poor		moderate		excellent

B. *Meeting knowledge gaps in specialized information.* How do you rate your skills in finding needed information, identifying occasional gaps in knowledge, and your openness to suggestions for further study?

1	2	3	4	5
poor		moderate		excellent

C. *Incongruity between yourself and teacher.* How do you rate your skills in handling the unavoidable disagreements which arise between consultants and other staff members? Some dimensions of the potential disagreement might include
   a. appraisal of problem seriousness
   b. amount of time and energy needed for remediation
   c. etiology, diagnosis, or identification of problem
   d. appropriate intervention strategies.

1	2	3	4	5
poor		moderate		excellent

D. *Territorial concerns between you and other support staff in building or system.* How do you rate your skills in identifying other resources in an organization, avoiding duplication of services, and striving to link existing services together for appropriate case management?

1	2	3	4	5
poor		moderate		excellent

E. *Ambivalence of your role as consultant.* How do you rate your skills in managing demands for direct service to children and providing appropriate consultation to staff?

1	2	3	4	5
poor		moderate		excellent

F. *Problem of being a student-consultant to staff member.* How do you rate your skills in getting beyond the student role (i.e., acting as professionally responsible as possible) and seeing organizational problems with a mature consultant perspective?

1	2	3	4	5
poor		moderate		excellent

G. Do you have any additional comments?

Consultees should be included on decision-making or policy-making boards overseeing both research and service functions. In this way, their best interests are represented and their commitment to the research may increase. In addition, the researchers' hypotheses are likely to become more sophisticated as a result of consultee input.

Allen, Chinsky, Larsen, Lockman, and Selinger (1976) reported on a study that involved consultation as one of its aspects. Their work is a good example of a balance between research and consumer needs. The articles by Emory Cowen and his associates (e.g., Cowen, 1973, 1977, 1980, 1982a, 1982b, 1983, 1984; Cowen, Dorr, Trost, & Izzo, 1972; Cowen & Gesten, 1978; Cowen, Lorion, & Dorr, 1974; Cowen, Trost, & Izzo, 1973; Zax et al.,

1966) are other fine examples of university service to the community resulting in high-quality research.

Final Evaluative Words

Consultants should collect data for only the following reasons:

* To help facilitate personal change;
* To help others change; or
* To help others make a decision.

Uninterpreted or thoughtlessly collected information wastes everyone's time. Information that is collected or used for punitive purposes is inappropriate for consultation service delivery or training. Emphases on strength and the capacities of people to change positively are in keeping with good consultation theory and practice.

SUMMARY

Consultants should construct an evaluation system to judge the value of their contributions to an organization. The evaluation approach can consider individual feedback to a consultant (e.g., from consultees and supervisors). In addition, evaluation can be planned to measure the effects of consultation on organizational dynamics and on links among organizations or organizational components that must collaborate to assist a client.

Trainers and practitioners can use evaluation methods to judge either their effectiveness as instructors or their readiness to consult. Many methodologies are available such as questionnaires, checklists, open-ended surveys, simulations, and treatment-oriented research (e.g., case studies of N-of-1 designs). The key consideration in evaluation is an understanding of how the data will be used to improve consultation service.

SUGGESTED READINGS

Cole, E., & Siegel, J. A. (Eds.). (1990). *Effective consultation in school psychology.* Toronto, Canada: Hogrefe & Huber Publishers.

Dougherty, A. M. (1990). *Consultation: Practice and perspectives.* Pacific Grove, CA: Brooks/Cole.

Hansen, J. C., Himes, B. S., & Meier, S. (1990). *Consultation: Concepts and practices.* Englewood Cliffs, NJ: Prentice-Hall.

Idol-Maestas, L., & Ritter, S. (1985). A follow-up study of resource/consulting teachers: Factors that facilitate and inhibit teacher consultation. *Teacher Education and Special Education, 8,* 121–131.

Kratochwill, T. R. (1985). Selection of target behaviors in behavioral consultation. *Behavioral Assessment, 7,* 49–61.

Mannino, F. V., Trickett, E. J., Shore, M. F., Kidder, M. G., & Levin, G. (1986). *Handbook of mental health consultation.* Rockville, MD: National Institute of Mental Health.

Martin, R. P., & Curtis, M. J. (1981). Consultants' perceptions of causality for success and failure of consultation. *Professional Psychology, 12,* 35–41.

Parsons, R. D., & Meyers, J. (1984). *Developing consultation skills.* San Francisco: Jossey-Bass.

West, J. F., & Cannon, G. S. (1988). Essential collaborative consultation competencies for regular and special educators. *Journal of Learning Disabilities, 21,* 388–408.

Chapter 7

The Consultant as Trainer

In-service or workshop training is not the same as consultation. Even flexibly formatted workshops have a body of preplanned information to impart to participants. In contrast, teaching within consultation is relatively unstructured and completely dependent on the issues raised by the consultees.

In-service training for school personnel or workshop training for other agencies is, however, often a valuable springboard for consultation. The workshop gives the consultant high visibility and, if it is well received, provides credibility, thereby increasing early approaches for service.

Consultants should not believe a single workshop or training experience will lead to significant behavioral changes on the part of the consultees. Even expertly done training is likely to create only a level of awareness on the part of trainees. Practice of new skills can be arranged during training, but application and generalization to the consultees' work settings require follow-up consultation.

The following is an overview of issues consultants might consider when planning workshops. The topics discussed have arisen in our training experiences and are meant to convey both some complex issues and mundane practical matters that affect the conduct of workshops.

ARRANGING THE TRAINING

Finding out what kind of training an agency desires or needs may be a straightforward or complex task. The consultant's base of operation (internal vs. external), the source of the request for training (grass roots vs. upper administration), the size of the agency, and the status of the agency (in crisis vs. coping well) are just a few of the parameters affecting the needs assessment problem.

Internal and External Consultants

If the consultants are internal, their training may fill a perceived need at the same time that it increases their credibility and visibility. From this base, the consultant can use a simple checklist form suggesting topics for training while leaving space for consultees to suggest other important topics. (See Appendix B for suggestions concerning potential in-service offerings.) Finding out potentially popular topics is probably easy for the internal consultant. Actually arranging the in-service training may be complicated.

When the idea for the training is generated by an internal consultant, he or she must make the arrangements for space and time and struggle to gain acceptability—inside resources are sometimes not as well identified or appreciated as those from somewhere else. This is probably why one of the common definitions of a consultant suggests that he or she must be from at least 50 miles away and arrive carrying a briefcase.

When consultants work with the same group of people all the time, it is probable that their weaknesses (usually irrelevant to the training area) become apparent to consultees. Externally based consultants have the advantage of greater control over what is known about them.

Scheduling Issues

School districts often have in-service days. Arranging time on one of these days simplifies planning because the district administrators have decided to free teachers from their regular duties while continuing to pay them. The disadvantage of using a district-wide in-service day is the possibility of large groups, relatively generic topics, and no provision for follow-up consultation. In lieu of established in-service times, consultants should consider the following options:

1. Freeing personnel from work for relatively short times through the use of aides or supervisors.
2. Rewarding personnel with graduate credit for attending evening or Saturday workshops.
3. Making attendance mandatory through administrative ruling, usually early morning or after work.
4. Adopting volunteer attendance during times suggested by the consultees.
5. Using written materials provided by the consultant to consultees, with no face-to-face group meetings.
6. Conducting ongoing, brief meetings with voluntary attendance as problem-solving sessions about a particular topic.

Each of these options has built-in costs and benefits. Some may not be considered possible in some settings, but all have been used in certain agencies. The existence of employee unions makes it unlikely that supervisors or administrators will require attendance just because the psychologist, resource teacher, social worker, or nurse says it is a good idea. This method guarantees an audience, but the consultant might experience all the resistance and hostility such a tactic engenders, thus decreasing the positive consequences of training. The consultant might be made the scapegoat for administrative arbitrariness.

As a general rule, volunteer audiences are much better than mandated audiences. It is impossible, however, to avoid completely (at least in education and business) training nonvolunteer audiences. It is possible and necessary to ascertain why people are present and strategize accordingly. Sometimes directly confronting the issue with some humor deflects the dissatisfaction with the mandatory attendance. For example, the consultant might say, "I felt wonderful watching all of you file in here, until _____ told me she was docking anyone who did not show. For a moment I thought my fame had preceded me. Now I *know* my fame has preceded me." Or the consultant can gaze out the window and say how hard it is to stay indoors on such a beautiful day, empathizing with the trainees. Ultimately, of course, a well-done workshop will engage all but the most resistant participant.

Arranging for graduate credit can be complicated but is often possible. Many school districts have arrangements with universities to give graduate or continuing education credits. University professors can arrange with their departments that a series of workshops will earn credit. Although this could result in tuition costs, some organizations pay for or have cooperative arrangements with the university regarding these charges.

Providing informative, written material about consultation services is unlikely to be influential in producing change, but it may trigger some consultation requests. In fact, the mere provision of training is unlikely to be influential unless follow-up consultation is available.

Volunteer attendance scheduled at times suited to the trainees is usually the optimal choice for the in-house consultant. This may result in small, variable groups but may also provide the most motivated audience. These groups are likely to spread the word of the consultant's helpfulness within the organization. Participants in such groups are often the most influential, competent teachers.

External consultants who are hired to do training avoid most of the arrangement complications. Rooms, audiovisual materials, and audiences are usually provided. On the other hand, external consultants may have difficulty identifying the exact training needs. They may lack intimate knowledge of a particular organization and can, therefore, unknowingly be used by a particular faction or the administration to promote an unpopular training package.

Needs Assessments

It is always wise to meet with key potential consumers of the training and learn their concerns. If distance makes this infeasible, some preparatory correspondence is helpful. In addition, consultants can use written needs assessment devices that break a particular topic area into its component parts, thus providing planning guidance.

A consultant must be sensitive to the fact that audiences will differ on their preferences for training. A delicate balance must sometimes be struck between satisfying the people who are paying for the training and the people who are taking the training. Consultants must never, however, conduct a training sequence that is merely an organization's propaganda unless they believe the propaganda. Personal enthusiasm and investment in the topic are critical for the success of such an endeavor.

Planning Summary

Consultants should consider the following list of important planning questions. New trainers may find that this is a helpful checklist of issues and things to do.

1. What is the source of the request?
   a. Administrative level
   b. Large- versus small-group problem
   c. Self- versus other-initiated
   d. Motive behind request
2. What topics are to be covered?
   a. Consultant expertise
   b. Needs assessment procedures
   c. History of problem(s) to be dealt with
   d. Key people already involved in the area
3. Where, when, for what, and whom?
   a. Voluntary versus nonvoluntary
   b. Credit versus noncredit
   c. Consultant fee or free of charge
   d. During working day or free time
4. Materials preparation
   a. Who types, duplicates, staples together, delivers?
   b. Who pays for these services?
5. Evaluation
   a. What variables will be identified for evaluation procedures?

   b. How will evaluation proceed?
   c. Who gets the results?
   d. What is information used for?
6.   Is the consultant expected to be available during meals (i.e., eat
     with participants) and after the training for evening consultations?
7.   Is there a procedure for evaluative data? All evaluative data should
     be shared.

IMPLEMENTATION

   Once the arrangements have been made and topics selected, the trainer's
second stage of work begins. There is no substitute for hard work and
preparation involving reading, audiovisual production, sequencing of activities, and scheduling. Some people are able to improvise. This process
usually fails, however, and participants feel indignant that their time was
wasted by an unprepared, disorganized, blatantly uninformed, or irrelevant trainer. Teachers, in particular, report that they have suffered through
some awful in-service training hours. Trainers should be prepared for
some direct challenges if trainees are unhappy with the focus of a workshop.

   Case Example. A well-known consultant and trainer reported that after only
   2 or 3 minutes of his opening comments to a group of school personnel, a
   woman stood up and said, "Is any of what you are about to say relevant to
   the practice of school social work? If not, tell me now and I won't waste my
   time." Although this request was jarring, it reflected at least some segment
   of the audience's disenchantment with required workshop training.

   Preparation does not imply overstructuring or overloading the participants. In fact, preparation (and some experience) allows for flexibility and
correct estimation of content domains that can be covered.
   Good training involves a particular body of information, appropriate
media support, and self-confidence about the topic. There is no need to be
a world-class expert. The key elements of implementation are the identification of the right amount of information to present, helpful audiovisual
devices for organization and/or impact, and a smooth sequencing of didactic and experiential or activity elements.

Amount of Information

   In terms of the amount of information, less is usually better than more.
Training participants tend to complain if they are overloaded and overwhelmed by information. They seem less likely to evaluate negatively if
they learn a few important, helpful facts. There are limits, of course, on
how little can be taught.

New learning that also demands new skills must be presented in small amounts with time allotted for practice. In the training of consultation skills, for example, it is common for participants to say they already do a lot of consulting. Role-play practice often reveals, however, how unskilled the participants are.

Another training strategy is to provide an overview of what the field contains. This is sometimes helpful in raising participants' awareness of what their training priorities should be. While raising the interest level, this strategy is not effective in teaching skills. If an organization development consultant provides an overview of effective organizational behavior, it is unlikely that the next staff meeting will be run any more skillfully than the previous one. The participants could realize, however, that there are possibilities for change.

Objectives and Competencies. In addition to carefully circumscribing content domain, the trainer should also develop an explicit list of targeted objectives or competencies. These might be made available to the participants. The trainer can then link the lecture and the activities to each of the competencies. This seems to increase participant willingness to engage in activities. The process of identifying training objectives also provides the participants with a standard against which to make helpful evaluations. No matter how careful the planning has been, there may be a participant who wanted more or different experiences. If the trainer's agenda is clear, it helps clarify the trainer's expectations of what comprises a successful training session and provides an avenue for input into the training experience.

It is frustrating to read at the end of 5 days of training that an important topic was omitted. Letting people know at the outset what will be covered and seeking their input immediately can reduce the probability of dissatisfaction.

Adapting the Workshop

A caveat is in order. Participants will sometimes try to change the content of a meeting because of their own anxieties or unresolved organizational difficulties. It is best not to overhaul a format until some quick, whole-group consensus has been discerned, perhaps through a write-in procedure. Then the change should come after a break in the action and be integrated smoothly with other planned activities.

Case Example. During workshop training on applied behavior analysis, a teacher aide kept pressing the trainer to devote the time to the discussion of individual, troublesome cases. The trainer's first response was to abandon the planned activities and move to a case consultation format. Fortunately, a co-presenter had picked up cues from the rest of the group that they preferred to learn an array of new techniques. The afternoon session was modified slightly to contain one case presentation with a group effort to identify antecedent and consequent conditions and to brainstorm potential strategies. The final evaluations indicated generally high satisfaction with the workshop.

Case Example. An unsuccessful outcome was measured after a workshop on consultation for social workers and psychologists at a children's center. The pretraining planning group insisted that the group needed conceptual, didactic inputs on consultation. The planning committee pointed out that real-life workloads made experiential elements and role-play redundant. The trainer reluctantly bowed to this analysis. During the 3 days of training, only two role-plays were introduced. These turned out to be the most popular parts of the training. The workshop, though generally well received, was criticized for information overload and not enough examples.

One of the evaluators described the planning error as the trainer "giving in to a group under stress," urging future workshop training to engage in more experiential learning that would develop cohesiveness in the staff.

The trainer should have realized the participants were fearful of encountering each other because of a poor organizational history. In fact, this group was a microcosm of the agency, a product of two recently merged systems, with the old guard and the new staff on uneasy terms over treatment philosophies and agency mission. These dynamics were unrelated to the training per se but had an effect on the entire training experience. It is important to stay flexible enough to modify a format or to give up "sacred cows" of training. It is equally important to be in charge of the training.

Audiovisuals

Audiovisuals can be helpful in training sessions if operated smoothly. Most universities offer courses in media production helpful for learning the basics such as operating the machinery. Such courses are also useful in teaching slide production and sequencing several media techniques in a single presentation.

Once the basics are mastered, there are still some important rules for media use, which beginners usually overlook.

1. Arrive early to check equipment, placement, and general room conditions.
2. Have all the collating accomplished before the presentation.
3. Include only one or two thoughts per slide or overhead transparency.

4. If the equipment breaks down during the training, seek help but be ready to go on quickly without it.
5. Handouts should be carefully planned as content supports and potential action sheets. They should be of excellent quality.

We have broken and/or disregarded each of these rules at some time and limped through training. With each infraction, however, we resolved never to be in the same situation again.

Case Example. When planning a workshop on aggressive children for 120 participants, all the important information was secured except for the shape of the room. When the trainers arrived, the overhead projector was in place, but the room was long, narrow, and windowless with only one light switch. The trainers were in total darkness or total brightness, rendering the overheads useless.

Handouts

Participants like to receive handouts that they can bring home and review at their leisure. Handouts should be plentiful, but not overwhelming, and provide sources of related or additional information. One helpful handout is a brief bibliography of readings. Another is a breakdown of target competencies and the schedule of training activities.

In addition to summaries of what the presenter has said, the handouts can be action oriented. Worksheets that can be used immediately on the job are particularly popular. Such handouts provide bridges between training and a change in work behavior.

The best method for distributing handouts is to assemble a training packet in a folder. The folder might have the participant's name on it or the name of the training topic. The trainer should not spend valuable time handing out material but should place it on a table for participants to retrieve.

If you must hand something out, go very slowly, starting at the same spot and specifying the route that the pages must take. Have just enough so that the person at the end is not deluged with extra pages—many of which will probably get lost.

It is very distracting to watch seven or eight pages being sent around with people checking with each other to see that they have all the appropriate information. Stop the action of the training to allow the distribution to occur. Do not be shy about asking for help from the audience to accomplish a distribution task. Allow them to worry about getting page 5 to someone in the eighteenth row! Very often people are happy to move around a little.

A final word on handouts and other visuals: At least some of them should be personalized for the group in some way. Using one overhead transparency with the schedule of the training, and another with the organizational system and subsystem names, for example, is helpful. Participants will appreciate that the trainer has done the requisite homework about the organization.

Use of sound effects in training depends on the quality of the original recording and the play-back equipment. Bad sound is worse than no sound. Participants become frustrated by not hearing or understanding a tape. Audio and videotapes can add dramatic elements to a presentation. Training dealing with child-related topics can be enhanced by tapes of a child in a classroom or in therapy.

Training experiences should be composed of somewhat diverse teaching strategies. Good lectures that are supported with good audiovisuals can keep the attention of a serious adult group for 1.5 to 2 hours and can give important basic information.

Participant Involvement

Many trainers use warm-up or ice-breaker activities to get the group relaxed enough to begin the experiential or participative part of the training process. Ice-breakers may be easy, fun activities or just a few words of personal information about the trainer.

If the trainer can establish a climate of trust and acceptance, the trainees will attempt almost any activity. The trainer does so as follows:

1. Sharing a relevant bit of personal information at the beginning of the session.
2. Sporadically sharing personal process concerns (e.g., "I'm worried that you're not understanding this.").
3. Treating the trainees with deference and respect.
4. Responding to feedback openly and nondefensively.
5. Learning names as quickly as possible.
6. Laughing at his or her own mistakes.

Participant-generated learning puts the participants in simulations of the problem or skill areas that were discussed in the lecture. Such small-group activities are invaluable but must relate to the participants' present situation and not be too anxiety provoking. The apparent relationship between the activity and the training goal is engineered through careful study of the participating organization and through linking knowledge domains with practice. The anxiety generated by the small-group exercise depends on who the participants are, the exercise, its timing, and the climate the trainer has established.

Risk. Some groups find role-playing easy, while other groups are frightened by it. Some groups are used to group simulations and need little introduction. It is usually true, however, that most people are a bit anxious about practicing new skills in front of others. Trainers can mitigate this anxiety by demonstrating role-play and by inquiring about the content and process of previous training events. This helps establish the experience level of the participants. The trainer must plan simulations that challenge the group but that do not overwhelm them.

Some exercises are frightening no matter what the experience level of the group. For example, telling participants to choose a group or partner using a process that involves the exclusion of some members is always anxiety provoking. The anxiety can be reduced if the trainer emphasizes the inclusion criteria rather than mentioning exclusion. Also it should be done in just 1 or 2 minutes so that nonselection into a group does not feel purposeful. Exercises involving feedback are also frightening, especially if they are unstructured. People are usually afraid of being rejected or being criticized in front of others.

Long exercises can be more troubling than short ones. If the trainer says to (a) think of what is important in a teammate, (b) interview those people who seem to have those qualities, (c) list top choices, (d) go back for another interview, and (e) choose a teammate, most of the participants are likely to be upset by this exercise.

Compare the aforementioned exercise with a statement such as, "You have just a minute. Find someone to work with you on some of the day's activities." The product (i.e., a teammate) is the same in both activities, but the overt need to accept one participant while rejecting others makes the first exercise more risky. With the increased risks may come concomitantly increased learning. If the learning is not doubled by doubling the risk, however, the anxiety generated may be a bad bargain.

Case Example. A weekend encounter group training exercise was entitled "Power and Rejection." The focus was on self-consciously building personal power and owning up to or increasing individual influence in a group. One of the exercises involved lengthy team-formation and team-building sessions. Suddenly, the trainers announced that one person from each group must be excluded. The exclusion process resulted in the formation of another group of rejects. Years after this training, at least one of the rejects reported carrying psychological scars. He said that he learned not to take part in such groups. Obviously, this was not the intended learning.

Timing. The trainer should decide in advance at which point in the training sequence to introduce a particular activity. Some trainers use a gradually increasing risk formula, while others immediately create a risky situation, thereby desensitizing the participants. The danger in the latter strategy is frightening some of the participants and placing them in upsetting situations that they would have experienced more easily later in the training session.

It is wise to plan some variety in the workshops. Didactic units can be followed by small-group, dyad, or individual activities. There is usually one long exercise. Participants report that it is easier to listen to a lecture in the morning and do activities in the afternoon. It is advisable, therefore, not to schedule the longest lecture during the last hour. A smooth flow among lecture, audiovisuals, small-group or individual activities, debriefing, discussion, and question-and-answer segments allows for different types of learners to experience a preferred mode for at least part of the training.

Humor

A few humorous remarks at the outset is a time-honored way to begin a speech. The goal of this is to put the audience in a favorable frame of mind for what will follow. Trainers probably should not tell jokes unless they tell jokes well. There is no point in beginning a training session by looking incompetent. More than jokes, however, participants appreciate spontaneous wit and a sincere nature.

It is never appropriate to use sarcastic or biting humor that takes advantage of a participant. A defensive, cautious stance will ensue. This is not an atmosphere conducive to learning. Other obvious pitfalls are off-color, sexist, or racist humor. The only person a trainer can safely derogate is himself or herself.

Final Implementation Notes

A trainer who moves around a room while speaking helps keep an audience's attention. Modulating voice tone and speed is also helpful in keeping participants alert. Trainers must be willing to be performers. A slightly exaggerated use of gestures and facial expressions is important in front of a group. The larger the group, the greater the effort should be to engage them. Eye contact and knowing names will keep a small group involved with a trainer. When the numbers climb over 30 or 40, however, the trainer must expend considerable energy just to make the participants focus on him or her. The media may not be the entire message, but it is influential, especially as a group grows.

The following is a checklist of implementation concerns. Trainers may want to review some of the classes they have given and those they have attended and alter the list to suit their preferences.

1. Housekeeping
   a. Provide schedule.
   b. Point out restrooms and/or refreshment
      availability.
   c. Allow 1½ hours for lunch, if possible.

2. Process
    a. Introduce new people (e.g., student observers).
    b. Clarify the trainers' roles (i.e., teacher, observer, facilitator).
    c. Avoid large-group confrontations if possible.
    d. Debrief with other leaders or observers during breaks.
    e. Divide leadership responsibilities clearly.
    f. Give one instruction at a time.
    g. Support participant risk taking.
3. Content
    a. Share goals.
    b. Tie activities to stated goals.
    c. Provide high-quality visual aids.
    d. Make paper and pencils available.
    e. Watch speech for jargon, sexist language, and off-color words.

EVALUATION

Throughout the entire planning and implementation phases of training, feedback and evaluative data are available. No training process is complete, however, without some sort of summative evaluation process.

Instruments

Like the other phases, the evaluation method may range from simple to complex. A simple yet effective device is shown in Table 7.1. The decisions regarding evaluation depend on audience comfort, time, and money.

Few people enjoy filling out long, cumbersome evaluations. If there is a reason that an evaluation instrument should be long or detailed, the trainer should explain the reason to participants.

Immediate Versus Delayed Evaluations. Evaluations are usually distributed immediately after the training session. There are two advantages to this method.

1. The participants are still somewhat captive, and therefore the return rate is high.
2. Immediate feedback is not contaminated by memory loss and gives the presenter a quick reading on his or her success.

The obvious problem with immediate feedback is that trainees are responding to the training session only and not to the usefulness of the training for on-the-job situations. Because the point of training is usually to improve performance in another setting, gathering delayed data is crucial. The time and expense of delayed data gathering often deters the trainer.

Table 7.1. Training Evaluation Instrument

---

1. Was the training relevant to your concerns?

   What new skill or knowledge will you
   implement?

   Would you seek further information on this
   topic?

2. Were the methods used effective?

   Lecture
   Role-plays
   Videotapes
   Simulations

3. Was the day well organized?

   Too much or too little information?

   Schedule too tight or not challenging enough?

4. What was the best part?

5. What was the worst part?

6. What are your suggestions?

Sometimes the usefulness of a training session can be measured indirectly by the number of invitations a trainer receives to work with the
original group. This seems a powerful, positive message; however, many
factors beyond the trainer's expertise can affect return engagements.

For example, the person arranging training sessions may accept another
position. This change in personnel can result in a new list of trainers. Or
an organization's training priorities may change because of external mandates. If new legislation, a new test, or a new instructional method comes
on the scene, even popular training sequences will be dropped in favor of
the new information.

If the trainer worked with a planning group before the training, it is
sometimes possible to meet with them again after the training to gather
follow-up data. This is also an indirect method but one that may lead to
further requests for training and consultation.

Follow-up

Perhaps the best training and evaluation method is an intensive presentation with follow-up sessions for a specific amount of time, 6 months to
2 years. Initially, the trainer gives participants concrete guidelines on how
to use the new skills and then arranges for observation periods. The trainer
may also set up small-group troubleshooting meetings over the course of

4 to 6 months to provide clarification and support of new behaviors. Such a training package is often attractive to organizations that are skeptical of the long-lasting value of one-shot training methodologies.

Another possibility is to arrange for feedback on new skills learned from taped examples. The trainer agrees to listen and provide feedback to the participants based on taped examples of the targeted training competencies. This can become cumbersome (i.e., tapes must be mailed and analyzed in a timely fashion), but is a possibility when distance makes follow-up visits infeasible.

SUMMARY

This chapter outlined the usefulness of training activities as part of a consultation program. Planning, implementation, and evaluation issues were discussed. Training done by consultants should be characterized by consultation processes. Trainers should involve participants at every phase, remain open and flexible in the face of feedback, learn from each experience, and leave the organization better able to meet its own needs rather than more dependent on outside resources.

SUGGESTED READINGS

Atkenson, B. M., & Forehand, R. (1978). Parent behavioral training: An examination of studies using multiple outcome measures. *Journal of Abnormal Child Psychology, 6,* 449–460.

Atkenson, D. M., & Forehand, R. (1979). Home based reinforcement programs designed to modify classroom behavior: A review and methodological evaluation. *Psychological Bulletin, 86,* 1298–1308.

Bergan, J. R., Neumann, A. J., & Karp, C. L. (1983). Effects of parent training on parent instruction and child learning of intellectual skill. *Journal of School Psychology, 21,* 31–39.

Brammer, L. M. (1985). *The helping relationship: Process and skills* (3rd ed.). Englewood Cliffs, NJ: Prentice-Hall.

Witt, J. C., Moe, G., Gutkin, T. B., & Andrews, L. (1984). The effect of saying the same thing in different ways: The problem of language and jargon in school-based consultation. *Journal of School Psychology, 22,* 361–367.

Zins, J. E., Curtis, M. J., Graden, J. L., & Ponti, C. R. (1988). *Helping children succeed in the regular classroom.* San Francisco: Jossey-Bass.

Appendix A

Consultation Transcripts

The following are annotated transcripts of consultation sessions. They are provided not because they represent perfect examples of consultation, but rather to give some further examples of consultation interactions that have been described in this book.

Each transcript represents consultation done at different operational levels or aimed at different targets. Some annotation has been added to highlight the verbal processes that illustrate important consultation processes.

We have disguised the transcripts to protect the identities of all involved, so they are not verbatim transcripts. They represent, however, accurate portrayals of real consultation sessions.

TRANSCRIPT I:
MICROLEVEL TARGET
WITH MESOSYTEM
INTERVENTION

These conversations represent portions of the first few meetings between a consultant (C) and a consultee (T).

Session I

C: Hi, I'm Bill Beaty.

T: I'm glad to meet you, Dr. Beaty. I've heard a lot about you.

C: Please, call me Bill. May I call you Joan? *(one-downsmanship)*

T: Oh, of course.

C: Is this a good time to meet about Joshua? I'm   *(rapport)*
free but can get back to you at another time if
this is not good.

T: Well, no. I can't meet now. In fact, I'm not
sure if we need to talk anymore. I went to my
principal and he said I might just as well refer
Josh for testing. I think I've tried everything.

C: It's up to you. I can stop back another time to   *(one-downsmanship, rapport)*
help you with the referral questions or with
some ideas about what to do while you wait for
the assessment to be done, or whatever you
would find most useful.

T: That's a good point. I'm sure the testing will
take 6 or 8 weeks at a minimum. I would like
you to stop by tomorrow at this time if you
could.

C: Fine. See you then.

Session II

C: I'm back. Tell me what's been happening   *(begin problem formulation)*
with Josh.

T: It's his attitude. He is incredibly rebellious. I
never see him agreeing to a command. He is
always arguing with me about what he has to
do and what he doesn't have to do. And his
mother joins right in apparently by telling him
he does not have to listen to me.

C: Sounds like you have at least two problems.   *(validation, summarizing)*
Josh and Mom.

T: Yes.

C: I'm sorry you're facing this. It makes it dou-   *(support, normalization)*
bly hard not to have parental support and I find
angry, rebellious kids can get on my nerves.

T: The truth is I'm getting kind of used to this.   *(is this a theme? teacher's*
Parents just don't help out like they used to.   *depression over changing*
When I began teaching, a child wouldn't dare   *times)*
complain to his parent about a teacher. He'd
pray his parent wouldn't find out about any
trouble because then he'd be in trouble at home
as well as at school.

C: I know what you mean. That's the way it   *(problem identification)*
worked in my house. Tell me more about Josh.
What is happening when you have him in
class? Give me some details of his behavior.

T: Well, he doesn't hand in work. He defies me
if I reprimand him or even if I just remind him
of the rules. He's used incredibly bad language
to me and to the children. It's strange, though,
at times he's a great kid. He seems very smart
in many ways but refuses to do academic work.
He lives with his mother who is very unpre-
dictable. She really doesn't have any more luck
in handling him than I do but has refused to
have him tested or get any kind of special education services. I think she's got a drug problem
or something pretty awful. His father is better
but does not have custody of him.

C: Our work in developing some classroom stuff   *(explain confidentiality,*
for Josh does not constitute any change in his   *parents' rights)*
program, so I think we're on safe ground in
talking about him in spite of the mother's concerns.

So Josh's major issues are refusal to hand in work, use of   *(summarize, identify*
defiant and obscene language, problems at home as well as   *problem)*
school, and general lack of cooperativeness. On the positive
side, he's smart and has a dad that might be an ally. I
don't know which area to start with. What problem seems
most central or most important to you?

T: That's a good question! They are all real bad.
I suppose if I could get him to hand in work, I
would at least feel that he's learning something.

C: So we might spend a little while discussing   *(make problem-solving*
just the work submission problem so that we   *process overt)*
can focus. Josh seems to have so many strikes
against him, I think it's a good idea to pull the
problem apart and see if we can find the thread
that might lead to some improvement. What
steps have you tried to increase his work?

T: I have kept him in from recess if he didn't
finish. I offered him some time at one of the
learning centers if he did finish. I sent notes
home to his mother and asked her to help him
with the work that wasn't done in school.

C: Have you seen even temporary improvement with any of these ideas? They certainly work with some children.

(reinforce teacher, analyze problem)

T: Yes. He doesn't like to be left behind at recess, but he'd just scribble something on his paper to get done and then get real belligerent if I asked him to do it right. He thinks that if he finishes a sheet that's all that's required. He doesn't care about the learning centers and his mom is really no help at all. If I write her a note, she may come in and act upset but be so scattered that it's almost scary.

C: So recess is important to him. What is his best subject? Is there a kind of work he is more likely to do than others or a subject he's actually good in?

(ignore comment about mother, stay with child problem for the moment)

T: He is better in math than other subjects and is actually a very good reader. I forgot to tell you that when he's with his father they go together to dirt bike racing. Josh rides those racing bikes—not motor bikes—the BMX racers, I think. He will rarely finish a math sheet but often has the first five or six problems done correctly.

C: How does Josh get along with older and younger children? I understood you to say that he has difficulty with his classmates.

(analyze problem with peers, widen circle of questions to include several spheres of Josh's life)

T: That's right. He's so sensitive and seems always to be looking for a fight. He's better with younger kids. I don't know about older ones. He's got a young half sister and is actually very loving toward her. I never see him pick on younger children on the playground, but I might be missing something.

C: So that's another group of possible strengths. He's good in reading and math if he tries. He has an activity he likes with his father that might serve as a reinforcer, and he may have better social skills with younger kids.

(focus on strengths, provide some data for possible intervention that is nonpunitive)

T: I haven't thought of him as having any strengths, to tell the truth. If you were in the classroom and getting attacked with his obscenities, these so-called strengths would be hard to remember.

C: I hear what you're saying! It is easier to think about something when I'm not in the middle of the emotional upset of it. It doesn't help that you've been dealing with this on your own for such a long time.   *(validation of teacher emotion, build referent power)*

T: You're right. The situation is emotional when he gets going with his bad language. Where does a kid learn language like that? And since his mother wouldn't agree to the special ed testing for the last 3 years, teacher after teacher is stuck with him with no help.

C: I think we have to find a way to get him working some more so he experiences some success and is less angry; have to involve his father rather than his mother; and have to talk over some strategies to use when he blows so that you are not caught with him out of control and the rest of the class looking on.   *(summarize, identify intervention targets)*

T: This is exactly what needs to happen, but I don't see how.

C: Well, let's look at what you know already. He is sometimes willing to do five or six math problems. Can he receive extra free time if he does six problems without complaining or making a scene when you assign the problems? He would have to be willing to do 6 for 3 days, then 7 for another 2 days, and then 8 until we got to about 10 with no outbursts.   *(summarize, introduce a strategy)*

T: I can talk to him one-on-one but never in front of the class. He will never cooperate when there's an audience. I'd have to arrange the program alone with him.

C: I think that's wise. He seems to need to show a scary face to his classmates. He may be afraid of them in some way.   *(reinforce teacher, reframe child's behavior)*

T: Where would he get the free time? He won't go to the centers. I can't leave him alone on the playground or send him out early by himself.

C: Is there a younger grade that goes before you? Could Josh be sent with the younger kids as a monitor of behavior when his behavior was especially good?   *(generate a plan)*

T: His fourth-grade teacher would not like him back even for a few minutes, I'm sure. But I could see if something could be arranged. It sounds complicated. I'd have to see him with the younger kids to feel comfortable with the idea.

C: Good point. I may be able to help. Perhaps I could observe him and let you know how he's doing along with reports from another teacher. Do you think a third- or second-grade teacher could use his help on the playground? *(reinforce teacher, offer to collaborate, analyze the plan)*

T: Everyone knows what a bad situation this is and would probably cooperate as long as there was no trouble.

C: That's a little pressure! I think we'd have to get some agreement going that relieved you of feeling completely responsible. *(make teacher's feelings of responsibility overt, offer to seek relief)*

T: Other teachers are already involved. He has Mr. Wells for social studies, Mrs. Hinks for PE, and Mr. Goldstein for science. If we all worked on this with the same program, it would feel pretty good.

C: Let's get these guys together and see if we can get some simple program going that makes it worth Josh's while to cooperate about work. I also think that we should see if we can contact his father and arrange for some cooperation from that source. Do you feel OK about contacting the father? Is there any problem with that? *(plan generation, case management)*

T: No, I don't think so. The dad has come in to teacher meetings before and is much better to talk with than the mom.

C: If all the teachers responded to his bad language in the same way (we'll have to decide what would be the best approach) and all the teachers gave him a chance to earn a little free time with good academic behavior, we might make some progress. I think getting the father involved is a key element. *(outline of plan goals)*

T: I would be so relieved never to have to speak to the mom again. You know I hate to say this, but I think she's really got some problems. I don't think she's completely sane.

C: That puts some of Josh's problems in per- *(address teacher concern* spective, I guess. I imagine he finds her difficult *about mom, use it to explain* to live with or that she has not been able to *Josh's behavior)* provide much consistent discipline. Having a custodial parent with mental health problems really puts a child at risk for serious problems as well.

T: I do feel sorry for Josh.

C: You are doing the right thing by working *(reinforce teacher action)* with his difficulties in a positive way. He will be in control of his free time with this idea we've been discussing, and that will be important.

Session III

C: Hi, Joan. What's happening in the fifth grade?

T: There's a lot going on, but one thing that's not happening are temper outbursts from Josh. An interesting thing happened. When I called the dad to ask for help with Josh, the dad told me that he was planning on seeking custody of Josh and that the continuing bad news from school had convinced him that he needed to have more contact with Josh. I can only think this is good news for Josh.

C: Has anything changed for Josh yet; that is, is *(problem analysis)* he spending more time with his dad already?

T: I think he is. I understand Josh told his mom that he wanted to live with his dad, and his mom got so mad she sent him over and he's been there all week.

C: That's interesting. What about you and *(follow-up on plan* Josh's other teachers? You and they were plan- *implementation)* ning on getting together to work out a common strategy with Josh. Did that happen?

T: Yeah. After we talked last week, I met with the team. We all agreed to ask Josh to do only a portion of his work and reward him with extra time with the second-grade recess. We also decided that if he blew his cool and used obscene language, we would escort him to the quiet room and ask him to come back when he

was ready. We haven't had to bring him to the
quiet room, but he has been earning a few minutes of extra recess every day.

C: I hope this is the start of some improvement   *(strategy generation)*
    for Josh. His home and classroom situations
    have changed. I think we should jump on the
    opportunity to let his dad know about the im-
    provement. Do you have time to call him and
    let him know?

T: He's coming by today for a report, so I can tell
    him then.

C: You're way ahead of me.   *(one-downsmanship)*

TRANSCRIPT II:
INDIVIDUAL AND GROUP
TARGETS WITH INDIVIDUAL
AND GROUP OPERATIONAL LEVELS

These are portions of consultation sessions between a consultant (C)
and a principal (P), and the consultant and a teacher committee (T).

P: I've heard about your work with Westside
    school and wanted to see if you'd be willing to
    do the same for my school.

C: I'm very flattered that you've heard good   *(problem identification)*
    things about me. I have loved working with the
    Westside staff. Every school is so different,
    though; what kinds of problems are you seeing
    among your staff?

P: I think *problem* might be too strong a word.
    This is a very strong staff—very experienced
    and dedicated to children.

C: They must be a pleasure to work with.   *(follow principal's lead;*
                                                        don't pathologize the staff)

P: Well, most of them really are, but there's
    some friction among them. This is my first year
    as principal, although I was assistant principal
    some years ago. In the meantime there's been a
    principal who initiated many changes, some of
    which were very unpopular with staff. He hired
    several people that were sympathetic to his
    program. Now he's gone, and the new people

feel threatened and the oldtimers think everything's going back to the way it was before Sam
was principal.

C: Wow! This is quite a situation for you to
inherit.

(empathy, validation)

P: It really is. A lot of these teachers know me
very well. I both taught here as well as being
the assistant principal. I think they feel they
will have a situation like years ago when every
teacher was his or her own person and there
was no need to collaborate and also no need to
adapt curriculum.

*(several issues are raised
here—principal's authority
with staff and staff
unwillingness to team and
to be responsive to a
changing population of
children)*

C: You seem to have a very good insight into the
dynamics of the situation. Tell me about the
issues between and among the teachers. What
do these look like?

*(problem identification on
first problem raised by the
principal; consultant is still
avoiding saying there are
any problems)*

P: You wouldn't believe some of the stuff. They
seem to disagree about everything—I mean if
one group says it's a good idea to do something,
I can almost guarantee another group will have
an objection. Some people will simply not talk
to one another. There's a problem in being supportive of different teaching styles. That is,
there's a lot of criticism of one another about
instruction.

C: So, the staff is rather untrusting of one another because of past events and is still trying
to establish a system in which there are good
guys and bad guys.

(summarize and reframe)

P: That's a good way to say it.

C: I think you will be able to have a lot of influence on this part of the dynamic because you
can be very open and accessible to both newcomers and oldtimers and not give either group
the upper hand in terms of influencing you on
an exclusive basis. If people find their group
identity is not a ticket to influence, sometimes
the need to stay stuck in a rigid group disap-
pears.

*(give power to principal;
emphasize his need to be
part of change process)*

P: I don't know if I follow you.

C: I did get a little carried away, didn't I? I guess I'm feeling optimistic because what you describe seems to have been fueled by some past administrative actions, and so I'm thinking your actions will be equally influential in the right direction.

(explain with continued emphasis on the principal's power)

P: Now, I wouldn't want you to get the impression I disagree with the previous principal's program. Quite the contrary, I think he was on the right track. We do have to accept teaming as a fact of life and have to accept that this school is not populated only by upper-middle-class, bright kids anymore.

C: I see. So a complication is that you have some of the same goals as the previous principal and need to find a way to implement a change process without causing the same furor as before. What makes it even more complex, perhaps, is that the experienced teachers may be expecting that you will be their ally, and the newer teachers are expecting to be left out in the cold.

(incorporate principal's concerns in a problem formulation and emphasize the difficulty of the situation facing the principal)

P: That's it, exactly. Now, how can you help us?

C: I would think we have to break the problem down into a few chunks. One is how you react to staff pressures to take sides and another is to identify what teachers see as the issues that face them. We have information from the organizational climate instrument they completed last year. Has that information ever been shared with them?

(problem-solving strategy made overt, seek information)

P: No.

C: An opening to the staff may be a feedback session to them on the issues they identified last year and then some problem solving about how to solve these issues. Is there a faculty committee that is assigned to working on the organizational climate?

(strategy generation; identify group that may be a bridge to the staff)

P: There is a group that helped choose the questionnaire last year. They have seen the printouts with the results but don't feel competent to interpret the results.

C: I wonder if I could talk with you some about how you handle the oldtimer versus newcomer split and be allowed to meet with this committee to ask their advice on how to approach the faculty? *(strategies—with principal and with staff)*

P: I think they would like to be involved. I should have asked them to join us today.

Before meeting with the teacher committee (T), the consultant was able to study the district's Teacher Opinionnaire—a questionnaire that was meant to measure such constructs as teacher rapport with principal, teachers' rapport with each other, satisfaction with special services, and so on. In this case, however, the computer printouts given to the consultant indicated that the district office had grouped items, not by their original scales, but in some idiosyncratic way. This made interpretation tenuous because the correlations of the items grouped together were low. In other words, it was unlikely that the scale, as redesigned by the teachers, was measuring the intended constructs.

Session II

T: We're very interested in understanding these printouts. Have you used this questionnaire before?

C: I have worked with schools that used this instrument, but you all asked for a rather unique analysis of the questionnaire. I see from the printout that you didn't go with the regular subscales or themes of the questionnaire but asked for analyses based on your putting the items together the way they made sense to you. That makes it a bit hard to understand, but it does individualize it to your particular situation. *(accept their previous work although it was not well conceived; reinforce their efforts)*

T: We worked with the district evaluation office on this and decided that we were more interested in some of the information than other parts.

C: To get a picture of what your faculty was trying to communicate, I've done an item-by-item analysis and picked out items that received very high or very low scores. I've also looked at the means, medians, and ranges of the responses to see where you all are in most *(give out a single sheet with areas of strength and concern ranked)* agreement and where there's a lot of diversity of opinion. Here's an overview of what I see as the issues the faculty picks out as special strengths of the situation here at Westside and those picked out as needing attention.

T: Boy, this is interesting. These are exactly what people are upset about.

C: Of course, this was filled out last May, and now you have a new principal. It strikes me that people may have different answers now.   *(problem analysis)*

T: Some things have changed, but a lot of the bad feelings that grew up over the past 3 years are still around. There's still a feeling of distrust among many of the faculty and an unwilling-ness to work together.

C: Of the issues that I have identified as coming from the faculty's questionnaire, which do you think is the most important one to work on— either a strength to enhance or a problem to overcome?   *(problem identification; prioritize)*

T: The thing that makes everyone upset is the decision-making process. Who gets to decide what? Who should be involved in the decision making? The confusion affects everyone.

C: Tell me more about this. Are there specific issues the faculty wants to be more involved in? Have there been particular problems?   *(identify problem; prioritize)*

T: Well, it's really everything. People don't know what the processes are for most deci-sions. We don't know if we are supposed to be involved. If a group works with students to plan something, sometimes other faculty mem-bers get upset if they are involved or affected by it at all without having been part of the decision making. It gets to be very upsetting.

C: So you see a pervasive confusion about the faculty's role in all decision making. What are the roles of the faculty standing committees? Do these groups play a part in the decision making in the school?   *(problem analysis)*

T: Good question. I'm not sure.

C: We might want to explore this, or maybe not.   *(one-downsmanship, overt*
I'm trying to understand the existing structure   *problem-solving process)*
to know how to explore the problem.

T: I don't think the committees are an important
piece of the problem. I think it's the faculty as
a whole. How we communicate with each other
and reach a point of decision. The principal is
a good guy, but he has not discussed these issues.

C: That's good input. I won't pursue the com-   *(reinforce input, begin to*
mittee structure. It may be that we need the   *develop a plan)*
principal's input on this.

Continued discussion with the group resulted in a plan to present the
faculty with some information about decision making; for example, distinctions among a faculty role to (a) receive decisions, (b) consult about
decisions, (c) have decision making delegated to them, or (d) participate in
the decision making. At the meeting, questions were posed about (a)
decisions made by the administrators, (b) decisions made by administrators after consultation with the faculty, (c) decisions made by the faculty,
and (d) decisions made by the faculty after consultation with administrators.

Following the brief input, the faculty was divided into groups to discuss
aspects of the school's decision making that were strong points and aspects
that were troublesome. Each of the groups took notes about their suggestions. These were collected by the consultant, summarized in writing a few
days after the meeting, and returned to the faculty for action.

TRANSCRIPT III:
INDIVIDUAL AND FAMILY TARGET
WITH MESOSYSTEM
INTERVENTION

This is an example of a consultant working at the behest of a family
from outside the school structure. The family has been working with the
community health or independent practice psychologist because the 7-
year-old boy, Sid, has been having trouble at home and at school. The
parents believe the major problem is the school. The family believes that
Sid's second-grade teacher is rigid and uncaring. The parents have had
unpleasant and unproductive meetings with the teacher. The parents report that Sid's teacher accuses Sid of being too much trouble in the classroom and resistant to her attempts to teach him. At home the parents view
Sid as mischievous, not doing what he is told all the time, but all in all a
"typical boy." The psychologist, Chuck, suggested that it would be helpful

for him to contact the school personnel, especially the teacher, to gain their cooperation in helping Sid. Chuck obtains a signed agreement that allows him to talk with the teacher and other school personnel. Because the family and Sid trust Chuck, they are pleased to give permission.

Chuck sends a letter to the teacher with one of the signed copies of the agreement from the family that allows the school personnel and Chuck to work together on Sid's difficulties:

Dear Ms. Flores:

I want to introduce myself because I'm working with one of your students, Sid, to help him do better at home and school. While his parents have been helpful describing his behavior at home, I wanted to enlist your expertise to help me understand his difficulties at school.

Included is a form that gives us permission from Sid and his parents to talk about the situation. I will give you a call to see if we can visit about this when it is convenient for you. I have worked with your principal, Betty Jones, with other children in your building. If you think it would be helpful, it would be great to include Betty and any others that you believe have an understanding of Sid's difficulties.

Thanks for your help!

Sincerely,

Chuck Clay, PhD
Psychologist

Four days later, Chuck (C) calls the teacher, Ms. Flores (T), to set up a time to visit.

C: Hello, Ms. Flores.
T: Yes . . .
C: Hello, this is Chuck Clay. I'm the psycholo- gist who has been working with your student, Sid, and his family. How are you?
T: Fine, thank you.   (guarded)
C: I was calling to set up a time that I could visit with you about Sid, if it is alright with you. Did you get my letter with the permission slip from Sid's parents?
T: Yes, I got the letter.
C: Great. I was hoping to find a time to meet that was good for you and anyone else you think would be helpful in giving me a better under- standing of Sid's problems at school.
T: Well, yes I did talk to Mrs. Jones about you, and she said that she would like to meet with

you also. How about Thursday after school, about 3 o'clock?

C: Let me see. I have an appointment then, but I will move it. Yes, that would work well. I'm really eager to get your help working with Sid. I keep feeling he isn't giving me the whole picture. *(laughing and demonstrating flexibility)*

T: Well, I imagine that is true. *(laughing also)*

C: Yes. . . . Well, thanks for setting up a time for me so soon. I look forward to meeting you in person. *(respecting teacher's busy schedule)*

T: OK. Goodbye, Dr. Clay.

C: Please, call me Chuck. Goodbye. *(one-downmanship)*

The goals of the first consultation visit are to seek cooperation, a problem description, and any ideas and suggestions for interventions, and to create openness for future input from the consultant. The overall purpose is to create an expectation of change in the teacher and subtly suggest that the teacher work with the child in a manner fitting Chuck's approach.

On Thursday afternoon, Chuck (C) meets the principal, Betty (P), and the teacher (T). Chuck is certain to arrive 5 minutes early and visit with the office receptionist.

C: Well, hello Betty. It's so good to see you again. How are you today? *(creating a friendly context)*

P: Hello, Chuck. I'm doing well today. It's good you weren't here yesterday, though. I want you to meet Anna Flores, Sid's teacher.

C: Hello, Anna. It's good to meet you in person.

T: Hello, Dr. Clay.

C: Oh, please call me Chuck. I really appreciate you taking the time to meet with me about Sid.

P: Well, Chuck, Sid has had some problems in school. He has not cooperated with us in his behavioral problems in the classroom, and his assignments continue to fall behind. His parents have called and visited with us, but we have made no progress.

C: It is really helpful for me to hear your views from the school perspective. By the way the parents and Sid talked, it seemed they were having trouble being objective about the situation. It was as if none of the problem was Sid's.

P: I think you've hit the nail on the head.

C: Oh, dear. That makes it so difficult when the parents can't understand their child's difficulties in school. I guess I'd lose a lot of business if all parents were good at cooperating with you!

P: Yes, I imagine so.

C: Anna, I was hoping that you could tell me some of the specific things that you have observed about Sid in the classroom that gets in his way of doing well?   *(asking for concrete problem descriptions)*

T: Well, basically Sid doesn't complete his work in class or at home. When I try talking with him about his work, he doesn't want to talk about it.

C: So, Sid isn't completing his work at school or home?   *(paraphrasing the segment that Chuck wants elaborated on and waiting for more information)*

T: Yes, Sid will sit and look out the window or play with a toy he sneaks into class. If I remind him to do his work, he sighs loudly and works for a while, but then he begins to daydream again.

C: It sounds like he can do the work but just isn't able to stay with the assignments to completion?

T: That is exactly right. But if he doesn't do his work, he will soon fall far behind.

C: Well, it's nice to hear that he hasn't fallen too far behind yet. We still might be in time to help Sid before this problem causes even bigger problems.

T: I hope so.

C: I have started working with his parents on the goal of helping Sid complete his assignments at home. Of course, no progress yet, but I'm hoping that if he can learn how to do it at home, it will help him at school.   *(sharing information to communicate a collaborative involvement)*

P: That would be a big help.

C: From what I can figure out from Sid and his parents, Sid doesn't get along well with the other children.   *(tentatively opening up another problem area)*

T: No, he doesn't have any friends that I have noticed. He doesn't talk with anyone in class.

C: How about at lunch or on the playground?

T: Sid will sit with the other children because they have to sit together. But I never see him visiting with the other kids. Likewise at PE, he doesn't visit with the other kids.

C: I was worried about his social abilities even though Sid's parents have seen only the grades as a problem. What do you think?

(creating collaborative context by treating teacher as expert while helping her to see another problem that she could help with if she recognizes it)

T: Yes, he doesn't talk or play with the other kids. I don't see him being mean to them like some other kids. He just doesn't seem to be very friendly.

C: This is very helpful to me. How do you think he feels most of the time? Can you tell me, or can you guess?

(finding out how teacher views the child; if the child is angry he gets less sympathy)

T: I'm not certain, because sometimes he just seems to be out of it, off in another world. But when I remind him of what he needs to get done, he seems angry.

C: I've noticed that when I talk to him about his school work, he gets tears in his eyes or maybe just a little watery. Has that occurred at school?

(creating a more caring stance toward Sid)

T: I'm not sure. Maybe . . .

C: Well, I'd appreciate your future thoughts on the tears. Sometimes children show anger more easily than sadness in depression. I'm just guessing that maybe this is happening with Sid. Of course, it's hard to be certain. The first approach I'm going to take with the parents is to help them structure Sid's time better so that he gets his work done. At the same time, I'm hoping to get them to interact more positively with him to help increase his good feelings about himself. Perhaps this will help him with confidence in doing his school work and learning to be social with friends. What do you think about this strategy?

(revealing an intervention that could hint at a parallel school intervention)

T: I really hadn't thought of his problems like that. . . . It sounds like a good idea.

C: You don't think I'm off base?

(collaboration with subtle pressure)

T: No, I don't think so.

C: Well, good. You know the way his parents act. They just aren't good at providing structure or warmth right now . . . it seems to me.

(furthering the separation of child from parents; attempting to increase positive feelings toward child)

T: Yes, I agree with that. I think you may be on the right track.

C: Well, thanks a lot for your thoughts. If you have any suggestions about helping him feel better about himself with his studies or friends, I'd appreciate the help.

T: I would be happy to help, but I'm not certain of what to do right now.

C: Thanks. I would appreciate any ideas that you may come up with. Please call me. I'll get back in touch with you in a couple of weeks to see how Sid is doing at school and let you know what is happening with us. Does that sound OK?

T: Sure, I'm certain that is fine.

When Chuck returns to his office, he writes a letter to the principal and the teacher to review issues and thank them for their support.

The strategy was for Chuck and the parents to help Sid be more cooperative at home initially. Then Chuck will approach the teacher with the same plan that has been discovered to be effective at home. The benefit of this approach is that the psychologist can make use of the parents' anger at the teacher and desire to help Sid as motivational forces toward change. The parents can feel satisfaction they discover how to help Sid and then "teach the teacher." By the time Chuck shares the plan with the teacher, the parents can be coaxed into a less angry state because they feel more in control of the situation.

Sid is having difficulty with friendships, gaining attention through negative behavior (otherwise his parents are inattentive), and he does not complete his homework or chores. Chuck discovers or labels Sid's acting-out behavior as signs of depression about not feeling good about himself academically or socially. The parents' are enlisted to help Sid learn how to gain attention through positive behaviors rather than negative behaviors.

Additionally, the parents help Sid complete his homework, arrange social activities, and develop friends.

After 2 weeks, Chuck sends a summary of Sid's and his parents' progress. As the parents and Chuck notice Sid's improvement at home, they become certain that the positive attention and structuring at home has lifted his depression, and his behavior is improving.

However, Sid still believes that his teacher does not like him, and he will not cooperate with her because of the way she acts toward him. Chuck recontacts Sid's teacher to arrange a meeting. Again, Chuck is flexible about setting up the time.

C: Anna, it's good to see you again. How is your day going?

T: Hello. Well, I'm sorry to keep you waiting. It's been a busy day.

C: I bet it has been busy. I've enjoyed sitting and watching the action around the office. Schools are very bustling places. *(avoiding blaming Anna for her tardiness)*

C: I was wondering how Sid has been doing with you?

T: Well, there has been improvement in his homework and getting his schoolwork done.

C: That is great. I'm really impressed with his progress. *(careful not to attribute change to self)*

T: Yes, I didn't think he would get this far.

C: Yeah, I was worried, too. I'm glad to hear he is doing better. What other kinds of concerns do you have about Sid?

T: He still seems to be unhappy here at school. He doesn't interact with his peers.

C: So, still no change in his social involvement. How does he do with you? Does he try to be friendly with you? *(making social issues Sid's so it will be easier to ask Anna to change without her feeling blamed)*

T: No, he doesn't seem to like me.

C: What would you think of us working together to get him to be more friendly with you and his peers?

T: That would be fine. What did you have in mind?

C: Oh, you mean how should we help him? Well, I was hoping we could develop an approach together. Is there any way you have worked with other kids that you prefer?

T: No, I've never tried to get a child to talk more; usually it's just the opposite!

C: I know what you mean. While we help him become better at being friendly, we need to be certain we don't overdo it!

T: That's right!

C: Maybe we could describe what we think is happening with him. What do you think are his biggest stumbling blocks to getting along better with his peers and you?

T: He doesn't even seem to try with the other kids, or with me.

C: You know that fits with what he says. He says that he is afraid that no one likes him.

T: He acts like he doesn't like anyone.

C: Hmmm, that is going to be difficult, then, isn't it? He pushes people away because he thinks they are going to push him away.

T: That is true. He just ignores people or acts pouty.

C: So, we need to show him he is wrong about being disliked. But you know by now he may have turned people against him.

T: Yes, I think you're right.

C: How would you feel about being the person who shows him he is wrong about being disliked? It may be too big a job for the other children in the beginning.

T: Sure, I feel fine about that, but I have 24 other children in class.

C: You certainly do. Sid can't expect all of your attention. Do you have any ideas about how to show Sid you like him that is so clear he can't miss it but at the same time does not use up much of your time?

T: Yes, I can get him to pass out the papers and supplies more often. He seems to like doing that.

C: That is a great idea! That would certainly be clear to him. You know something that seemed to mean a lot to him was when I patted him on the back or shoulder. What would you think of patting him and telling him he is doing a good job, when he is?

T: That sounds easy enough.

C: I should tell you I stole that idea from a teacher at Hartley Elementary. A teacher there told me that if she just patted a child on the back and said "good job" five times a day, it really made a big difference. It would be interesting to know if that would have any effect on Sid.

T: I'm happy to try that. It won't take much time, and I could do it with a few other kids so the other kids don't feel left out and Sid won't be suspicious.

C: That's a good point. I'll have to tell that to the teacher at Hartley. Well, let's see. Our first goal is to get Sid to believe that people aren't against him. Perhaps then he will be more willing to be friendly himself. You will allow him to pass out materials more often and pat him, saying "good job" about five times a day. Does that sound OK?

T: That sounds easy. I hope it helps.

C: Well, I'm sure we can think of other things to do if it doesn't, but I hope it works, too. I will be talking with him about being more friendly and be certain that he notices what you do.

T: OK.

C: So, can I call you in a week to see how this is going? I'd like to get to meet with Sid after you have worked with him for a week.

T: That sounds fine.

Chuck talks with Sid about his teacher, saying that she did like him but she did not believe he liked her. Chuck told Sid that he told his teacher that Sid really likes her. Now Sid can see what happens when a teacher thinks that Sid will be friendly. As Sid continues to make changes, Chuck continues to consult with Sid's teacher.

Appendix B

In-service Options for Consultants

The following is a list of possible topics for workshops or consultation sessions.

Teaching to student needs
    Developing instructional alternatives for individual learners
    Diagnostic teaching
    Structuring space for classroom control
    Structuring time

Learning centers
    Designing centers
    Setting up centers
    Introducing students to centers
    Record keeping

Contracts
    Writing academic and behavioral objectives
    Advisor conferences with students
    Writing contracts
    Evaluating and modifying contracts

Peer and cross-age tutoring
    Selecting tutors and students to be tutored
    Training tutors
    Materials and activities for tutoring
    Supervision and evaluating the tutoring
    Developing a learning-through-teaching program for an entire class

Affective education
    Integrating affective goals with academic tasks
    Creative expression
    Raising self-esteem in students
    Encouraging self-expression in students
    Human development program ("magic circle" group technique)
    Cooperative classroom program
    Role-playing
    Experiential and value clarification exercise
    Bibliotherapy
    Teacher advisory conferences with students
    Materials and media for effective education

General classroom management
    Setting up rules, expectations, consequences
    Establishing routines
    General classroom management strategies
    Monitoring systems: teacher, peer, self
    Class courts
    Stimulating student involvement

Social relations in the classroom
    Assessing your classroom (sociograms and other measures)
    Interventions to promote social relationships
    Intervening in social problem situations

Behavior modification
    Identifying appropriate behaviors to be reinforced in children
    Identifying inappropriate behavior to be changed
    Using praise systematically
    Using varied reward systems
    Rewarding individual students
    Rewarding groups of students
    Peer reinforcement
    Planned ignoring
    Using behavior checklists
    Evaluating and revising the behavior modification system

Punishment
    Knowing when to punish
    Knowing how to punish
    Combining rewards and punishments
    Withdrawing rewards and privileges
    Time-out procedures

In-class suspension
In-school suspension
Early dismissal plan

Crisis intervention
General procedures
Reality therapy
Responding to specific problems
Attention seeking
Testing limits
Withdrawn behavior
Social immaturity
Hyperactivity
Aggressive behavior
Negativism: defiance and work refusal
Lying and cheating
Stealing
Sexual acting out
Antiauthoritarian behavior
Bizarre behavior
The scapegoat
Phobias
Absenteeism

Ethnic studies
Cultural differences in learners
Capitalizing on a child's ethnic background in the classroom
Language
Family experience
Community experience
Developing positive ethnic self-concept
Cultural awareness
Art
Music
Literature
Food
Dress
History
Ways to involve the community and parents in school
Understanding your feelings about different ethnic groups
Identifying stereotypes
Values clarification in relation to ethnic issues

Other areas for schools
    Developing interpersonal relationships
    Facilitating communication
    Defining goals and priorities
    General problem solving
    Setting discipline procedures and codes

Other areas for teacher teams
    Developing interpersonal relationships
    Facilitating communication
    Defining goals and priorities
    General problem solving
    Setting discipline procedures and codes
    Giving and taking feedback

Other areas for teachers
    Value clarification
    Meeting teacher needs
    Setting goals for change
    Assessing your teaching
    Personalizing your classroom
    Developing helping skills
    Developing interpersonal communication
    Coping with stress

References

Alinsky, S. D. (1946). *Reveille for radicals*. Chicago: University of Chicago Press.

Allen, G. J., Chinsky, J. M., Larsen, S. W., Lochman, J. E., & Selinger, H. V. (1976). *Community psychology and the schools*. Hillsdale, NJ: Lawrence Erlbaum Associates.

American Psychological Association. (1979). *Ethical standards of psychologists*. Washington, D.C.: American Psychological Association.

Apter, S. J. (1982). *Troubled children/Troubled systems*. Elmsford, NY: Pergamon Press.

Apter, S. J., & Conoley, J. C. (1984). *Childhood behavior disorders and emotional disturbance: An introduction to teaching troubled children*. Englewood Cliffs, NJ: Prentice-Hall.

Argyris, C. (1971). *Management and organizational development*. New York: McGraw-Hill.

Baker, B. N. & Wilemon, D. L. (1977). Managing complex programs: A review of major research findings. *R&D Management, 8*(1), 23–28.

Bandura, A. (1986). *Social foundations of thought and action: A social cognitive theory*. Englewood Cliffs, NJ: Prentice-Hall.

Barker, R. G. (1978). *Habitats, environments, and human behavior*. San Francisco: Jossey-Bass.

Barker, R. G. & Gump, P. V. (1964). *Big school, small school*. Stanford: Stanford University Press.

Bennis, W. G. (1969). *Organization development: Its nature, origins, and prospects*. Reading, Mass.: Addison-Wesley.

Bergan, J. R. (1977). *Behavioral consultation*. Columbus, OH: Bobbs Merrill.

Bergan, J. R., & Kratochwill, T. R. (1990). *Behavioral consultation in applied settings*. New York: Plenum Publishing.

Bergan, J. R., & Neumann, A. J. (1980). The identification of resources and constraints influencing plan design in consultation. *Journal of School Psychology, 18,* 317–323.

Bergan, J. R. & Tombari, M. L. (1975). The analysis of verbal interactions occurring during consultation. *Journal of School Psychology, 13,* 209–226.

Bergan, J. R., & Tombari, M. L. (1976). Consultant skill and efficiency and the implementation of outcomes of consultation. *Journal of School Psychology, 14,* 3–14.

Berlin, I. N. (Ed.). (1975). *Advocacy for child mental health*. New York: Brunner/Mazel.

Biklen, D. (1974). *Let our children go: An organizing manual for parents and advocates*. Syracuse, N.Y.: Human Policy Press.

Biklen, D. (1976, March). Advocacy comes of age. *Exceptional Child,* pp. 308–313.

Blake, R. R. & Mouton, J. S. (1976). *Consultation*. Reading, Mass: Addison-Wesley.

169

Blake, R. R. & Mouton, J. S. (1978). Toward a general theory of consultation. *Personnel and Guidance Journal, 56,* 328–330.

Borich, G. D. (Ed.). (1974). *Evaluating educational programs and products.* Englewood Cliffs, New Jersey: Educational Technology Publications.

Brickman, P., Rabinowitz, V. X., Karuza, J., Jr., Coates, D., Cohn, E., & Kidder, L. (1982). Models of helping and coping. *American Psychologist, 37,* 368–384.

Browne, P. J., Cotton, C. C. & Golembiewski, R. T. (1977). Marginality and the O. D. practitioner. *The Journal of Applied Behavioral Science, 13*(4), 493–505.

Burns, M. L. (1977). The effects of feedback and commitment to change on the behavior of elementary school principals. *Journal of Applied Behavioral Science, 13,* 159–166.

Campbell, J. (1968). *The hero with a thousand faces.* Princeton, N.J.: Princeton University Press.

Campbell, J. (1974). *The mythic image.* Princeton, N.J.: Princeton University Press.

Caplan, G. (1970). *The theory and practice of mental health consultation.* New York: Basic Books.

Chalfant, J. C., Pysh, M. V, & Moultrice, R. (1979). Teacher assistance teams: A model for within-building problem solving. *Learning Disability Quarterly, 2,* 85–96.

Chandy, J. (1974, August). *The effects of an inservice orientation on teacher perception and use of the mental health consultant.* Paper presented at the annual meeting of the American Psychological Association, New Orleans, LA.

Christensen, K. C., Birk, J. M., Brooks, L., & Sedlacek, W. E. (1976). Where clients go before contacting the university counseling center. *Journal of College Student Personnel, 17,* 396–399.

Christensen, K. C. & Magoon, R. N. (1974). Perceived hierarchy of helpgiving sources for two categories of student problems. *Journal of Counseling Psychology, 21,* 311–314.

Cleven, C. A., & Gutkin, T. B. (1988). Cognitive modeling of consultation processes: A means for improving consultee's problem definition skills. *Journal of School Psychology, 26,* 379–389.

Conoley, C. W., Conoley, J. C., Ivey, D., & Scheel, M. (in press). Enhancing consultation by matching the consultee's perspectives. *Journal of Counseling and Development.*

Conoley, J. C. (1981a). Advocacy consultation: Promises and problems. In J. C. Conoley (Ed.), *Consultation in Schools: Theory, research, procedures.* New York: Academic Press.

Conoley, J. C. (1981b, August). *Advocacy versus organization development: Consultation training dilemmas.* Paper presented at the Annual Meeting of the American Psychological Association. Los Angeles, CA.

Conoley, J. C. (1989). Professional communication and collaboration. In M. Reynolds (Ed.), *Knowledge base for the beginning teacher* (pp. 245–254). Washington, DC: American Association of Colleges of Teacher Education.

Conoley, J. C., Apter, S. J. & Conoley, C. W. (1981). Teacher consultation and the resource teacher: Increasing services to seriously disturbed children. In F. Wood (Ed.), *Perspectives on a new decade* (pp. 111–126). Reston, VA: Council for Exceptional Children.

Conoley, J. C., & Conoley, C. W. (1982). *School consultation: A guide to practice and training.* Elmsford, NY: Pergamon Press.

Conoley, J. C., & Gutkin, T. B. (1986a). Educating school psychologists for the real world. *School Psychology Review, 15,* 457–465.

Conoley, J. C., & Gutkin, T. B. (1986b). School psychology: A reconceptualization of service delivery realities. In S. N. Elliott & J. C. Witt (Eds.), *The delivery of psychological services in schools: Concepts, processes, and issues* (pp. 393–423). Hillsdale, NJ: Lawrence Erlbaum Associates.

Conoley, J. C., & Haynes, G. (in press). Ecological perspectives. In R. D'Amato & B.

Rothlisberg (Eds.), *Quest for answers: A comparative study of intervention models through case study.* White Plains, NY: Longman Publishing.

Cormick, G., & Love, J. J. (1976). Ethics of interventions in community disputes. In H. Kelman, D. Warwick, & G. Bermant (Eds.), *Ethics of social intervention.* New York: John Wiley & Sons.

Cossairt, A., Hall, R. V., & Hopkins, B. L. (1973). The effects of experimenter's instructions, feedback and praise on teacher praise and student attending behavior. *Journal of Applied Behavior Analysis, 6,* 89–100.

Cowen, E. L. (1973). Long-term follow-up of early detected vulnerable child. *Journal of Consulting and Clinical Psychology, 41*(3), 438–446.

Cowen, E. L. (1977). Baby-steps toward primary prevention. *American Journal of Community Psychology, 5,* 1–22.

Cowen, E. L. (1980). The wooing of primary prevention. *American Journal of Community Psychology, 8,* 258–284.

Cowen, E. L. (1984). Training for primary prevention in mental health. *American Journal of Community Psychology, 12,* 253–259.

Cowen, E. L. (1982a). Help is where you find it: Four informal helping groups. *American Psychologist, 37,* 385–395.

Cowen, E. L. (1982b). Primary prevention research: Barriers, needs and opportunities. *Journal of Prevention, 2,* 131–137.

Cowen, E. L. (1983). Primary prevention in mental health: Past, present, and future. In F. D. Felner, L. A. Jason, J. N. Moritsugu, & S. S. Farber (Eds.), *Preventive psychology: Theory, research, and practice* (pp. 11–25). Elmsford, NY: Pergamon Press.

Cowen, E. L., Dorr, D., Trost, M. A., & Izzo, L. D. (1972). A follow-up study of maladapting school children seen by non-professionals. *Journal of Consulting and Clinical Psychology, 39,* 235–238.

Cowen, E. L., & Gesten, E. L. (1978). Community approaches to intervention. In B. B. Wolman, J. Egan, & A. O. Ross (Eds.), *Handbook of treatment of mental disorders in childhood and adolescence* (pp. 102–123). Englewood Cliffs, NJ: Prentice-Hall.

Cowen, E. L., Lorion, R. P., & Dorr D. (1974). Research in the community cauldron: A case history. *The Canadian Psychologist, 15*(4), 313–325.

Cowen, E.L., Trost, M.A., & Izzo, L.D. (1973). Nonprofessional human-service personnel in consulting roles. *Community Mental Health Journal. 9*(4) 335–341.

Cummings, T. G. (1980). *Systems theory for organizational development.* New York: John Wiley & Sons.

Curtis, M. J., Curtis, V. A., & Graden, J. L. (1988). Prevention and early intervention through intervention assistance programs. *School Psychology International, 9*(4), 257–264.

Cutler, R. L., & McNeil, E. B. (1964). *Mental health consultation in schools: A research analysis.* Ann Arbor: Department of Psychology, University of Michigan.

deCharms, R. (1976). *Enhancing motivation: Change in the classroom.* New York: Irvington.

Deci, E. L., Nezlek, J., & Sheinman, L. (1981). Characteristics of the rewarder and intrinsic motivation of the rewardee. *Journal of Personality and Social Psychology, 40,* 1–10.

de Shazer, S. (1985). *Keys to solution in brief therapy.* New York: W W Norton.

Elliott, S. N., Witt, J. C., Galvin, G., & Peterson, R. (1984). Acceptability of behavior interventions: Factors that influence teacher's decisions. *Journal of School Psychology, 22,* 353–360.

Ellis, A., & Grieger, R. (1977). *Rational-emotive therapy: Handbook of theory and practice.* New York: Springer.

Ellis, A. & Harper, R. A. (1975). *A new guide to rational living.* Englewood Cliffs, N.J.: Prentice-Hall.

Erchul, W. P. & Chewning, T. G. (1990). Behavioral consultation from a request-centered relational communication perspective. *School Psychology Quarterly*, 5(1), 1–20.

Fairchild, T. N. (1976). School psychological services: An empirical comparison of two models. *Psychology in the Schools*, 13(2), 156–162.

French, J. R. P., & Raven, B. (1959). The bases of social power. In D. Carwright (Ed.), *Studies in social power* (pp. 230–301). Ann Arbor: University of Michigan Press.

French, W., & Bell, C. H. (1978). *Organization development* (2nd ed.). Englewood Cliffs, N.J.: Prentice-Hall.

Friedman, M. P. (1978, April). *Mental health consultation with teachers: An analysis of process variables.* Paper presented at the annual meeting of the National Association of School Psychologists, New York, NY.

Friend, M. (1984). Consultation skills for resource teachers. *Learning Disability Quarterly*, 7, 246–250.

Friend, M. (1985). Training special educators to be consultants: Considerations for developing programs. *Teacher Education and Special Education*, 8, 115–120.

Fuchs, D. & Fuchs, L. S. (1989). Exploring effective and efficient prereferral interventions: A component analysis of behavioral consultation. *School Psychology Review*, 18(2), 260–283.

Gallessich, J. (1973). Organizational factors influencing consultation in schools. *Journal of School Psychology*, 11, 57–65.

Gallessich, J. (1974). Training the school psychologist for consultation. *Journal of School Psychology*, 12, 138–149.

Gordon, E.W. (1982). Human ecology and the mental health professions. *American Journal of Orthopsychiatry*, 52(1), 109–110.

Goldstein, A. P. (1981). *Psychological skill training.* Elmsford, NY: Pergamon Press.

Graden, J. L., Casey, A., & Christenson, S. L. (1985). Implementing a prereferral intervention system: I. The model. *Exceptional Children*, 51(5), 377–384.

Gresham, F.M., & Kendell, G.K. (1987). School consultation research: Methodological critique and future research directions. *School Psychology Review*, 16, 306–316.

Gutkin, T.B. (1981). Relative frequency of consultee lack of knowledge, skill, confidence, and objectivity in school settings. *Journal of School Psychology*, 19, 57–61.

Gutkin, T.B., & Conoley, J.C. (1990). Reconceptualizing school psychology from a service delivery perspective: Implications for practice, training, and research. *Journal of School Psychology*, 28, 203–223.

Gutkin, T.B., & Curtis, M.J. (1990). School-based consultation: Theory and techniques. In T.B. Gutkin & C.R. Reynolds (Eds.), *The handbook of school psychology* (2nd edition. New York: John Wiley & Sons.

Gutkin, T. B., Henning-Stout, M. & Piersel, W. C. (1988). Impact of a district-wide behavioral consultation prereferral intervention service on patterns of school psychological service delivery. *Professional School Psychology*, 3(4), 301–308.

Haley, J. (1977). *Problem-solving therapy.* San Francisco: Jossey-Bass.

Halpin, A., & Croft, D. (1963). *The organizational climate of schools.* Danville, IL: Interstate Printers & Publishers.

Hattie, J. A. & Sharpley, C. F. & Rogers, H. J. (1984). Comparative effectiveness of professional and paraprofessional helpers. *Psychological Bulletin*, 95(3), 534–541.

Hayman, J. L., & Napier, R. N. (1975). *Evaluation in the schools: A human process for renewal.* Belmont, Calif.: Wadsworth.

Henning-Stout, M., & Conoley, J. C. (1987). Consultation and counseling as procedurally divergent. *Professional Psychology*, 18, 124–127.

Hobbs, N. (1982). *The troubled and troubling child.* San Francisco: Jossey-Bass.

Hoffman, L. (1981). *Foundations of family therapy: A conceptual framework for systems change.* New York: Basic Books.

Horwitz, A. (1978). Family, kin and friend networks in psychiatric help-seeking. *Social Science and Medicine, 12,* 297–304.

Hughes, J., & Hall, R. (Eds.). (1989). *Handbook of cognitive-behavioral interventions in the classroom.* New York: Guilford Press.

Hyman, I. (1975). The school psychologist and child advocacy. In G. Gredler (Ed.), *Ethical and legal factors in the practice of school psychology.* Harrisburg, Pa.: Pennsylvania Dept. of Education.

Idol, L., Nevin, A., & Paolucci-Whitcomb, P. (1986). *Models of curriculum-based assessment.* Rockville, MD: Aspen Publications.

Idol, L., Paolucci-Whitcomb, P., & Nevin, A. (1986). *Collaborative consultation.* Rockville, MD: Aspen Publications.

Idol, L. & West, J. F. (1987). Consultation in special education: II. Training and practice. *Journal of Learning Disabilities, 20*(8), 474–494.

Idol-Maestas, L. (1983). *The special educators consultation handbook.* Rockville, MD: Aspen Publications.

Isaacson, D. (1981). *An investigation into the criterion related validity of the consultation analogue situation.* Unpublished doctoral dissertation, Syracuse University.

Katz, D., & Kahn, R. L. (1978). *The social psychology of organizations* (2nd ed.). New York: John Wiley & Sons.

Kazdin, A.E. (1980a). Acceptability of alternative treatments for deviant child behavior. *Journal Applied Behavior Analysis, 13,* 259–273.

Kazdin, A.E. (1980b). Acceptability of time-out from reinforcement procedures for disruptive child behavior. *Behavior Therapy, 11,* 329–344.

Kazdin, A. E. (1981). Acceptability of child treatment techniques: The influence of treatment efficacy and adverse side effect. *Behavior Therapy, 12,* 493–506.

Kazdin, A.E. (1982). The token economy: A decade later. *Journal of Applied Behavior Analysis, 14,* 331–346.

Kazdin, A.E. & Cole, P.M. (1981). Attitudes and labeling biases toward behavior modification: The effects of labels content, and jargon. *Behavior Therapy, 12,* 56–68.

Kegan, R. (1982). *The evolving self: Problem and process in human development.* Cambridge, MA: Harvard University Press.

Kelly, G.A. (1963). *A theory of personality: The psychology of personal constructs.* N.Y.: W W Norton.

Kohlberg, L. (1964). The development of moral character and moral ideology. In M. Hoffman & L. Hoffman (Eds.), *Review of child development research (Vol. 1).* New York: Russell Sage.

Kounin, J. S. (1970). *Discipline and group management in classrooms.* New York: Holt, Rinehart & Winston.

Lambert, N. M., & Cole, L. (1977). Equal protection and due process considerations in the new special education legislation. *School Psychology Digest, 6*(4), 11–12.

Larrivee, B. (1985). *Effective teaching for mainstreaming.* New York: Longman.

Lawrence, P. R., & Lorsch, J. W. (1969). *Developing organization: Diagnosis and action.* Reading, Mass.: Addison-Wesley.

Lentz, F.E., & Shapiro, E.S. (1986). Functional assessment of the academic environment. *School Psychology Review, 15,* 346–357.

Lepper, J. R., & Greene, D. (1978). *The hidden costs of rewards.* Hillsdale, NJ: Lawrence Erlbaum Associates.

Levine, M., & Levine, A. (1970). *A social history of helping services: Clinic, court, school and community.* New York: Meredith.

Lewin, K. (1951). *Field theory and social science.* New York: Harper & Row.

Lippitt, R. & Lippitt, G. (1975). Consulting process in action. *Training and Development Journal, 29,* 48–54.

Mannino, F. V. (1969). *An experience in consultation as perceived by consultants and consultees.* Adelphi, Md.: Mental Health Study Center, National Institute of Mental Health.

Mannino, F. V., & Shore, M. F. (1979). Evaluation of consultation: Problems and prospects. In A. S. Rogawski (Ed.), *Mental health consultation in community settings. New directions for mental health services.* San Francisco, Calif.: Jossey-Bass.

Martens, B. K., Lewandowski, L.J., & Houk, J.L. (1989). Correlational analysis of verbal interactions during the consultative interview and consultees' subsequent perceptions. *Professional Psychology: Research & Practice, 20*(5), 334–339.

Martens, B.K, Peterson, R.L., Witt, J.C., & Cirone, S. (1986). Teacher perceptions of school-based interventions. *Exceptional children, 53,* 213–223.

Martin, R.P. (1978). Expert and referent power: A framework for understanding and maximizing consultation effectiveness. *Journal of School Psychology, 16,* 49–55.

Martin, R. P. (1983). Consultant, consultee, and client explanations of each others behavior in consultation. *School Psychology Review, 12,* 35–41.

Massachusetts Advocacy Center and Massachusetts Law Reform Institute. (1975). *Making school work.* 2 Park Square, Boston, Mass.

Matuszek, P. A. (1981). Program evaluation as consultation. In J. C. Conoley (Ed.), *Consultation in schools: Theory, research, procedures.* New York: Academic Press.

McCready, K. F. (1985). Differentiation of transference versus theme interference in consultee-centered case consultation. *School Psychology Review, 14,* 471–478.

McKinley, J. B. (1973). Social networks, lay consultation and help-seeking behavior. *Social Forces, 51,* 275–292.

Mearig, J. S. (1974). On becoming a child advocate in school psychology. *Journal of School Psychology, 2,* 121–129.

Mearig, J. S. (1978). *Working for children: Ethical issues beyond professional guidelines.* San Francisco: Jossey-Bass.

Medway, F. J. (1979). How effective is school consultation. A review of recent research. *Journal of School Psychology, 17*(3), 275–282.

Meyers, J. A. (1973). A consultation model for school psychological services. *Journal of School Psychology, 11,* 5–15.

Meyers, J. (1975). Consultee centered consultation with a teacher as a technique in behavior management. *American Journal of Community Psychology, 3,* 111–121.

Meyers, J., Parsons, R. D., & Martin, R. (1979). *Mental health consultation in schools.* San Francisco: Jossey-Bass.

Minuchin, S. (1974). *Families and family therapy.* Cambridge, MA: Harvard University Press.

Minuchin, S., Rosman, B. L., & Baker, L. (1978). *Psychosomatic families: Anorexia nervosa in context.* Cambridge, MA: Harvard University Press.

Newland, T. E. (1981). School Psychology—Observation and reminiscence. *Journal of School Psychology, 19*(1), 4–20.

Norris, D.A., Burke, J.P., & Speer, A.L. (1990). Tri-level service delivery: An alternative consultation model. *School psychology quarterly, 5,* 89–110.

Olson, D.H., Russell, C.S., & Sprenkle, D.H. (1983) Circumplex model of marital and family systems: VI. Theoretical update. *Family Process, 22,* 69–83.

Patterson, G.R., Reid, J.B., Jones, R.R., & Conger, R.E. (1975). *A social learning approach to family intervention, Volume 1: Families with aggressive children.* Eugene, OR: Castalia Publishing Co.

Phillips, B.N. (1990). *School psychology at a turning point.* San Francisco: Jossey-Bass.

Piersel, W. C., & Gutkin, T. B. (1983). Resistance to school-based consultation: A behavioral analysis of the problem. *Psychology in the Schools, 20,* 311–326.

Pipes, R. B. (1981). Consulting in organizations: The entry problem. In J. C. Conoley (Ed.), *Consultation in schools: Theory, research, procedures.* Academic Press: New York.

Pryzwansky, W. B. (1974). A reconsideration of the consultation model for delivery of school based psychological services. *American Journal of Orthopsychiatry, 44,* 579–583.

Pryzwansky, W. B. (1977). Collaboration or consultation: Is there a difference? *Journal of Special Education, 11,* 179–182.

Pryzwansky, W. B. (1986). Indirect service delivery: Considerations for future research in consultation. *School Psychology Review, 15,* 479–488.

Rae-Grant, Q. (1972). The art of being a failure as a consultant. In J. Zusman & D. L. Davidson (Eds.), *Practical aspects of mental health consultation.* Springfield, Ill.: Charles C. Thomas.

Reimers, T.M., Wacker, D.P., & Koeppl, G. (1987). Acceptability of behavioral treatments: A review of the literature. *School Psychology Review, 16,* 212–227.

Reschly, D.J. (1988). Assessment issues, placement litigation, and the future of mild mental retardation classification and programming. Special Issue: Emerging challenges. *Education and Training in Mental Retardation. 23* (4), 285–301.

Reynolds, M. (1979). *A common body of practice for teachers: The challenge of public law 94–142 to teacher education.* Minneapolis: National Support Systems Project.

Reynolds, M. (1989) (Ed.), *Knowledge base for the beginning teacher.* Washington, DC: American Association of Colleges of Teacher Education.

Rhodes, W. C. (1967). The disturbing child: A problem of ecological management. *Exceptional Children, 33* (7), 449–455.

Rhodes, W. C., & Tracy, M. L. (1972). *Study of child variance.* Ann Arbor: University of Michigan Press.

Ritter, D. R. (1978). Effects of a school consultation program upon referral patterns of teachers. *Psychology in the Schools, 15* (2), 239–243.

Robbins, P. R., & Spencer, E. C. (1968). A study of the consultation process. *Psychiatry, 31,* 362–368.

Robbins, P. R., Spencer, E. C., & Frank, D. A. (1970). Some factors influencing the outcome of consultation. *American Journal of Public Health, 60,* 524–534.

Rosenfield, S. (1987). *Instructional consultation.* Hillsdale, NJ: Lawrence Erlbaum Associates.

Salmon, D. & Lehrer, R. (1989). School consultant's implicit theories of action. *Professional School Psychology, 4* (3), 173–187.

Sarason, E. K., & Sarason, S. B. (1969). Some observations of the introduction and teaching of the new math. In F. Kaplan & S. B. Sarason (Eds.), *The psycho-educational clinic: Papers and research studies* (pp. 91–108). Boston: Massachusetts State Department of Mental Health.

Sarason, S. B. (1982). *The culture of the school and the problem of change* (2nd ed.). Boston: Allyn & Bacon.

Sarason, S. B. (1981). An asocial psychology and a misdirected clinical psychology. *American Psychologist, 36* (8), 827–836.

Sarason, S.B., & Doris, J. (1979). *Educational handicap, public policy, and social history.* New York: Free Press.

Sarason, S. B., Levine, M., Goldenberg, I. I., Cherlin, D. L., & Bennett, E. M. (1960).

Psychology in community settings: Clinical, educational, vocational, social aspects. New York: John Wiley & Sons.

Schein, E. H. (1969). *Process consultation.* Reading, MA: Addison-Wesley.

Schein, E.H. (1990). Organizational culture. *American Psychologist, 45,* 109–119

Schmuck, R. A. (1976). Process consultation and organization development. *Professional Psychology, 7,* 626–631.

Schmuck, R. A., & Runkel, P. (1985). *The handbook of organization development in schools* (3rd ed.). Palo Alto, CA: Mayfield Publishing Company.

Schowengerdt, R., Fine, M., & Poggio, J. (1976). An examination of some bases of teacher satisfaction with school psychological services. *Psychology in the Schools, 13,* 263–274.

Secord, P. F., & Backman, C. W. (1974). *Social Psychology* (2nd ed.). New York: McGraw-Hill.

Sibley, S. (1986). *A meta-analysis of school consultation research.* Unpublished doctoral dissertation, Texas Woman's University, Denton, TX.

Skinner, B. F. (1974). *About behaviorism.* New York: Knopf.

Steele, F. (1973). *Consulting for organizational change.* Amherst, Mass.: Univ. of Mass. Press.

Stein, D. D. (1972, April). *Training needs in clinical psychology.* Paper presented in symposium at the Annual Meeting of the Eastern Psychological Association. Boston, Mass.

Swap, S.M., Prieto, A.G., & Harth, R. (1982). Ecological perspectives of the emotionally disturbed child. In R.L. McDowell, G.W. Adamson, & F.H. Wood (Eds.), *Teaching emotionally disturbed children.* Boston: Little, Brown.

Tannenbaum, R., & Schmidt, W. H. (1958). How to choose a leadership pattern. *Harvard Business Review, 36,* 95–101.

Taylor, S. (1979). *Negotiation: A tool for change.* D. D. Rights Center of the Mental Law Project.

Taylor, S. J., & Biklen, D. (1979). *Understanding the law: An advocate's guide to the law and developmental disabilities.* Under H.E.W., Office of Human Development Grant of National Significance #54P71332/3-01, Syracuse University and The Mental Health Law Project.

Tharp, R. G., & Gallimore, R. (1985). The logical status of metacognitive training. *Journal of Abnormal Child Psychology, 13,* 455–466.

Tombari, M. L., & Bergan, J. R. (1978). Consultant cues and teacher verbalizations, judgments, and expectancies concerning children's adjustment problems. *Journal of School Psychology, 16,* 212–219.

Tyler, F. B., Pargament, K. I., & Gatz, M. (1983). The resource collaborator role: A model for interactions involving psychologists. *American Psychologist, 38,* 388–398.

Tyler, M. M., & Fine, M. J. (1974). The effects of limited and intensive school psychological teacher consultation. *Journal of School Psychology, 12,* 8–16.

von Bertalanffy, L. (1968). *A systems view of man.* Boulder, CO: Westview Press.

Watzlawick, P., Weakland, J., & Fisch, R. (1974). *Change.* New York: W W Norton.

West, J. F., & Idol, L. (1987). School consultation (Part 1): An interdisciplinary perspective on theory, models, and research. *Journal of Learning Disabilities, 20,* 388–408.

White, P. L., & Fine, M. J. (1976). The effects of three school psychological consultation modes on selected teacher and pupil outcomes. *Psychology in the Schools, 13,* 414–420.

Wilcox, M. R. (1977, August). *Variables affecting group mental health consultation for teachers.* Paper presented at the annual meeting of the American Psychological Association, San Francisco, CA.

Witt, J. C. (1986). Teachers' resistance to the use of school-based interventions. *Journal of School Psychology, 24,* 37–44.

Witt, J. C., & Elliott, S. N. (1983). Assessment in behavioral consultation: The initial interview. *School Psychology Review, 12,* 42–49.

Witt, J.C. & Elliott, S.N. (1985). Acceptability of classroom management strategies. In T.R. Kratochwill (Ed.), *Advances in school psychology*. (Vol. 4, pp. 251–288). Hillsdale, N.J.: Lawrence Erlbaum.

Witt, J.C., Elliott, S.N., & Martens, B.K. (1984). Acceptability of behavioral interventions used in classrooms: The influence of amount of teacher time, severity of behavior problem, and type of intervention. *Behavioral Disorders, 9*(2), 95–104.

Witt, J. C., & Martens, B.K. (1983). Assessing the acceptability of behavioral interventions used in classrooms. *Psychology in the Schools, 20*, 510–517.

Witt, J. C., & Martens, B. K. (1988). Problems with problem-solving consultation: A re-analysis of assumptions, methods, and goals. *School Psychology Review, 17*, 211–226.

Witt, J. C., Martens, B. K., & Elliott, S. N. (1984). Factors affecting teachers' judgments of the acceptability of behavioral interventions: Time involvement, behavior problem severity, and type of intervention. *Behavior Therapy, 15*, 204–209.

Witt, J.C. & Robins, J.R. (1985). Acceptability of reductive interventions for the control of inappropriate child behavior. *Journal of abnormal child psychology, 13*, 59–67.

Wolf, M.M. (1978). Social validity: The case of subjective measurement of how applied behavior analysis is finding its heart. *Journal of applied behavior analysis, 11*, 203–214.

Woolfolk, R.C. & Woolfolk, A.E. (1979). Modifying the effect of the behavior modification label. *Behavior therapy, 10*, 5–578.

Ysseldyke, J.E., & Christenson, S. (1986). *The Instructional Environment Scale*. Austin: Pro-Ed.

Ysseldyke, J.E., & Christenson, S. (1987). *The Instructional Environment Scale*. Austin, TX: Pro-Ed.

Zax, M., Cowen, E. L., Izzo, L. D., Madonia, A. J., Merinda, J., & Trost, M. A. (1966). Teacher-aide program for preventing emotional disturbances in young school children. *Mental Hygiene, 50*, 406–415.

Author Index

179

Subject Index

About the Authors

Jane Close Conoley received her doctoral degree in School Psychology from the University of Texas at Austin in 1976. Her practice, research, and writing efforts have focused on treatment of children with emotional disturbance in the context of the systems in which they live, particularly schools and families.

Dr. Conoley is a frequent lecturer and consultant to mental health organizations and schools. She works with groups on team development, problem solving, and managing the interpersonal and environmental stresses that pervade work and family life. She is particularly well known for her analyses of consultation as a method of delivering mental health services. She is editor of the *Mental Measurements Yearbook* series and the author and editor of seven books concerning measurement and child and family mental health needs. In addition, she has written numerous articles and chapters concerning consultation, family therapy, and professional issues in school psychology.

Jane is a past president of the Division of School Psychology of the American Psychological Association and has been a faculty member in psychology departments at Syracuse University and Texas Woman's University and psychologist for the Burleson Special Education Cooperative. She is currently professor and chair of the Department of Educational Psychology at the University of Nebraska at Lincoln and a regular consultant to several schools in Nebraska.

Collie Wyatt Conoley received his doctoral degree in Counseling Psychology from the University of Texas at Austin in 1976. His practice and research has included children and adults. The majority of his scholarly activity has involved examining the application of systems theory through consultation and family and individual counseling.

Collie has continued to develop his understanding of consultation through applied practice and research. He has spent 10 of his postdoctoral years in applied settings and 4 years in academic settings. He has worked in community mental health centers, a university counseling center, a children's psychological center, and independent practice. He was a faculty member at the University of North Texas and currently teaches at the University of Nebraska at Lincoln. He is an associate professor, director of the Counseling Psychology training program, and director of the Psychological and Educational Services Clinic.

DATE DUE

AG 21 '99			
OC 08 '99			
DEC 1 6 1999			
1/30/00			
SE 08 00			
10/29/01			
10/19/02			

GAYLORD   PRINTED IN U.S.A